HIGHER PAY IN HARD-TO-STAFF SCHOOLS

The Case for Financial Incentives

Cynthia D. Prince

A SCARECROWEDUCATION BOOK
Published in partnership with the
American Association of School Administrators

The Scarecrow Press, Inc.
Lanham, Maryland, and Oxford
2003

A SCARECROWEDUCATION BOOK
Published in partnership with
the American Association of School Administrators

Published in the United States of America
by Scarecrow Press, Inc.
A Member of the Rowman & Littlefield Publishing Group
4501 Forbes Boulevard, Suite 200, Lanham, Maryland 20706
www.scarecroweducation.com

PO Box 317
Oxford
OX2 9RU, UK

British Library Cataloguing in Publication Information Available

Library of Congress Cataloging-in-Publication Data

Prince, Cynthia D.
  Higher pay in hard-to-staff schools : the case for financial incentives /
Cynthia D. Prince.
      p. cm.
  "Published in partnership with the American Association of School
Administrators."
  Includes bibliographical references (p.   ).
  ISBN 0-8108-4696-9 (Paperback : alk. paper)
  1. Teachers—Salaries, etc.—United States. 2. Teacher turnover—United
States. 3. Rewards and punishments in education—United States. 4. Incentive
awards—United States. I. Title.
LB2842.22 .P75 2003
331.2'813711'00973—dc21

                                                          2002154368

To Christopher and Allison

CONTENTS

v

FOREWORD

One of the most important issues facing school system leaders today is attracting quality teachers and principals to schools that serve large concentrations of poor, minority, and low-achieving students. Record teacher shortages, combined with increased expectations that schools will bring all students to high levels of performance, have created tough challenges for educators and policymakers alike. We know that student achievement is directly affected by the quality of students' classroom teachers. It follows that quality teachers and principals should characterize schools serving students with the greatest needs.

However, schools that serve large concentrations of poor and minority students experience the greatest difficulty attracting and keeping highly qualified teachers. The *No Child Left Behind Act* has created an even greater sense of urgency for school system leaders to address this problem because school districts must ensure that every teacher is highly qualified within the next four years or face federal sanctions. The question is how.

Critics of public education believe that using public funds to enable parents to flee low-performing schools will ensure that every child has access to a high-quality teacher. This book proposes a better alternative: invest public dollars to attract exemplary teachers and principals to the nation's most challenging schools and improve working conditions in these schools so that teachers will not want to leave. Instead of requiring parents to hunt for quality schools for their children, let's ensure quality educators in every neighborhood school.

Paul D. Houston
Executive Director
American Association of School Administrators

ACKNOWLEDGMENTS

I would like to thank the following individuals for reviewing earlier versions of this manscript and for providing many thoughtful comments and suggestions: Joe Schneider; Honor Fede; Anne Turnbaugh Lockwood; Terri Schwartzbeck, Jay Goldman and Judy Seltz, American Association of School Administrators; Michael Podgursky, University of Missouri, Columbia; Allan Odden, University of Wisconsin, Madison; and Marcie DiAnda, Rob Lao, and Denise McKeon, National Education Association. Thanks go to Liz Core for providing administrative assistance. Special thanks go to Mark Mazur for innumerable contributions to this document. Although I am indebted to the reviewers for their assistance, the views presented are mine and do not necessarily reflect those of the reviewers or their organizations.

INTRODUCTION

How to close the academic achievement gap between rich and poor may well be the most complex—and the most intractable—problem that school system leaders face. A seemingly endless list of strategies has been proposed to close the achievement gap: smaller classes, smaller schools, standards-based reform, whole-school reform, lengthening the school day, lengthening the school year, before- and after-school programs, vouchers, charter schools, and greater parental involvement. The most drastic strategies include privatizing the management of public school systems, mayoral and state takeovers, and school reconstitution.

But one idea has received scant attention in discussions of reform strategies: redistributing the best teachers and principals to the lowest performing schools. No strategy to improve student achievement is likely to work in the absence of highly qualified teachers and strong, supportive principals who can create good working conditions that will attract and retain them. Yet mounting evidence shows that poor and minority students are increasingly segregated not only by race and poverty, but also by access to quality teachers. The more segregated the school, the more likely that students in the school will be taught by underprepared and inexperienced teachers.

For the past year the American Association of School Administrators has been examining what it will take to attract exemplary teachers and principals to the nation's neediest schools, a long-standing problem made even more pressing by new federal laws requiring that every teacher be highly qualified. This book addresses this complex issue.

A previous paper, *The Challenge of Attracting Good Teachers and Principals to Struggling Schools,* was released by AASA in January 2002.[1] It addressed a simple question: Why don't school districts simply assign the most effective educators to the schools that serve children with the greatest needs? Compelling research evidence indicates that teacher quality is the single most important school variable affecting student achievement, yet tremendous disparities exist in student access to well-qualified teachers. The more impoverished and racially isolated the school, the greater the likelihood that students will be taught by inexperienced teachers, uncertified teachers, and out-of-field teachers who do not hold a degree in the subject they are assigned to teach. Examples from the paper include:

Disparities in teacher experience
- Placement in difficult assignments without adequate support is one of the chief reasons beginning teachers give for leaving the profession. Yet novice teachers with three years of classroom experience or less are twice as likely to be assigned to high-minority, high-poverty schools.[2]
- Even within districts, experienced teachers are not equitably distributed. In Baltimore, where there is relatively little variability in poor and minority student enrollment among the city's public schools, inexperienced teachers are still concentrated in enclaves of schools with the highest proportions of poor and minority students and the lowest levels of achievement.[3] Staffing patterns in Philadelphia look very similar.[4]

Disparities in teacher preparation, knowledge, and skills
- In California, more than 40,000 classroom teachers were teaching on emergency permits or waivers in 1999–2000. Low-achieving schools were nearly five times as likely as high-achieving schools to employ these teachers; high-minority schools were nearly seven times as likely as low-minority schools to employ them.[5]

- In Illinois, teachers in schools with the highest proportions of poor, minority, and low-performing students were five times more likely to have failed at least one teacher competency test than teachers in the state's most affluent schools. Nearly one-fifth of Chicago teachers tested between July 1988 and April 2001 failed at least one teacher test—3.5 times the suburban teacher failure rate.[6]

Disparities in teacher turnover

- Teacher shortages are usually attributed to rising student enrollments, class-size reduction, teacher retirements, and resignations. But about half of the overall turnover of teachers is migration from one school to another. Schools that report difficulty attracting teachers are nearly twice as likely to have higher than average rates of teacher turnover.[7]
- Teachers in schools with minority enrollments of 50 percent or more migrate at twice the rate of teachers in schools with relatively few minority students.[8]

In sum, teacher shortages are not caused primarily by failure to produce enough teachers. Experts on teacher supply and demand acknowledge that with the exception of some high-need areas such as mathematics, science, and special education, the number of teachers who are certified each year is sufficient to meet demand.[9] Even in California, where more than 40,000 classroom teachers were teaching on emergency permits or waivers in 1999–2000, the state's Commission on Teacher Credentialing estimated that there were enough credentialed teachers in the state to fill every teaching vacancy four times over.[10]

The primary problems are inadequate retention and uneven distribution of quality teachers—there simply are not enough well-qualified teachers willing to work in poor schools. High-achieving, affluent school districts seldom encounter problems filling teacher and administrator vacancies. School systems with high concentrations of poor and minority students, on the other hand, must generally make do with much smaller pools of qualified applicants. In 1996–1997, for example, the Baltimore City Public Schools (the poorest school system in Maryland) received 1,800 applications for 826 teacher vacancies, an average of just over 2 applications per job opening. In comparison, Montgomery

County Public Schools (the wealthiest school district in Maryland) received 6,109 applications for 665 teacher vacancies, an average of 9 applications per job opening. Even though Montgomery County had 20 percent fewer vacancies than Baltimore, the district received more than 3 times as many applications. Baltimore would have had to hire nearly half of those who applied in order to fill all of its vacancies. Montgomery County, on the other hand, needed only to cream the top 11 percent from its considerably larger pool of teacher applicants.[11]

The same pattern is noted for school administrators. Poor schools encounter much greater difficulty attracting principals than more affluent schools do, even within the same district. In 1997–1998, for example, the New York City Public Schools had 123 openings for principals. The average number of applicants per elementary school vacancy was 40, but in 30 percent of the schools with vacancies, no more than 20 candidates applied. The school with the fewest applicants (11) was P.S. 92, a school located in a poor neighborhood of Brooklyn. The school with the most applicants (116) was P.S. 223 in Queens. (Within the same Queens district, however, only 21 applications were submitted for a job opening at a school in a high-poverty neighborhood.)[12]

Differences in community wealth can make enormous differences in a school district's ability to recruit and retain highly qualified educators. Less affluent districts complain that neighboring districts routinely raid their best teachers and principals with promises of higher salaries and better working conditions. But while salary differentials may partially explain inequities in teacher quality across districts, they are wholly inadequate explanations for inequities in teacher quality *within* districts. A number of political and bureaucratic barriers within districts contribute to the problem, such as:

- seniority clauses in union contracts that allow veteran teachers to choose where and whom they will teach;[13]
- state policies that prevent principals and other hiring authorities from obtaining information on teachers' failure rates on certification tests;[14]
- district policies that grant central office staff, rather than principals, the authority to select teachers from applicant pools;[15] and

- cumbersome internal district procedures that hinder qualified veteran teachers from transferring to low-achieving schools.[16]

Changing these kinds of dysfunctional policies and procedures will require politically astute superintendents who are willing to take risks that will inevitably create conflict. For example:

- If superintendents concentrate the best teachers in the lowest-performing schools to give disadvantaged students the best chance to excel, they run the risk of alienating parents in the district's more affluent schools and accelerating middle-class flight.
- If superintendents reassign or remove unqualified teachers and principals in an effort to improve failing schools, they may draw the ire of union officials, parents, and school board members. In some cases, removing existing staff may be a futile gesture anyway. As one former teacher in East Los Angeles pointed out, "Replacing the teachers is an empty threat. Nobody's waiting for our jobs."[17]
- In many districts, superintendents have difficulty keeping experienced teachers in needy schools because union contracts allow teachers with seniority to transfer to more desirable schools. Superintendents must carefully weigh whether the benefit of having the authority to decide where teachers and principals are allowed to work is worth the risk of losing experienced staff to neighboring districts.
- Recent articles in the *New York Times* and the *Washington Post* document cases of teachers retiring early, switching schools, or changing the subjects or grades they teach in an effort to avoid the pressures, and sometimes single-minded focus on testing, created by high-stakes state tests.[18] How can superintendents attract qualified teachers and principals to their district's lowest-performing schools when state rewards and sanctions tied to student test scores loom as powerful disincentives?

What will it take to overcome these problems and attract exemplary teachers and principals to the nation's most challenging schools? This question eventually led to a proposed solution and this book. This book argues that the approach that holds the greatest promise of attracting and retaining highly qualified educators in the nation's neediest schools is to offer targeted financial incentives to those willing to take on more difficult assignments. Evidence suggests that targeted financial incentives can increase the relative attractiveness of these jobs and overcome teacher reluctance to work in hard-to-staff schools.

Chapter 1 examines what we know about the effectiveness of using financial incentives as a policy remedy to attract and retain highly qualified teachers in high-poverty, low-performing schools. This section presents the equity arguments and the economic arguments for financial incentives, and describes where the teachers' unions stand on this issue. Chapter 2 reviews a wide array of incentive programs that states, districts, businesses, and the federal government are currently offering to attract and retain teachers, particularly in high-poverty, low-performing schools and in designated teacher shortage areas. Chapter 3 presents nine lessons learned from incentive programs that have been tried and provides insights as to how incentives should be structured to increase the likelihood that they will be effective.

NOTES

1. Prince, C. (2002, January). *The challenge of attracting good teachers and principals to struggling schools*. Arlington, VA: American Association of School Administrators. www.aasa.org/issues_and_insights/issues_dept/challenge.htm.

2. Bolich, A. M. (2000). *Reduce your losses: Help new teachers become veteran teachers*. Atlanta: Southern Regional Education Board. www.sreb.org/main/highered/reducelosses.asp.

3. Maryland State Education That Is Multicultural Advisory Council. (1998, September). *Minority achievement in Maryland: The state of the state*. Baltimore: Maryland State Department of Education. www.msde.state.md.us/minority/pdf_files/minority.pdf.

4. Watson, S. (2001, May). *Recruiting and retaining teachers: Keys to improving the Philadelphia Public Schools*. Philadelphia: University of Pennsylvania, Consortium for Policy Research in Education. www.cpre.org/Publications/children01.pdf.

5. The Center for the Future of Teaching and Learning. (2000). *Teaching and California's future: The status of the teaching profession 2000. An update to the Teaching and California's Future Task Force.* Santa Cruz, CA: Author. www.cftl.org/documents/2000complete_report.pdf.

6. Rossi, R., B. Beaupre, & K. Grossman. "5,243 Illinois teachers failed key exams." *Chicago Sun-Times*, September 6, 2001. www.suntimes.com/output/news/cst-nws-main06.html; Grossman, K., B. Beaupre, & R. Rossi. "Poorest kids often wind up with the weakest teachers." *Chicago Sun-Times*, September 7, 2001. www.suntimes.com/output/news/cst-nws-main07.html.

7. Ingersoll, R. (2001, January). *Teacher turnover, teacher shortages, and the organization of schools.* Seattle: University of Washington, Center for the Study of Teaching and Policy. www.depts.washington.edu/ctpmail/PDFs/Turnover-Ing-01-2001.pdf.

8. National Center for Education Statistics. (1998). *The condition of education.* Washington, D.C.: U.S. Government Printing Office. Cited in Haycock, K. (2000, Spring). "No more settling for less." *Thinking K–16,* 4(1), 3–12. Washington, D.C.: The Education Trust.

9. Darling-Hammond, L. (2000). *Solving the dilemmas of teacher supply, demand, and standards: How we can ensure a competent, caring, and qualified teacher for every child.* New York: National Commission on Teaching & America's Future. www.nctaf.org/publications/solving.pdf; Strauss, R. (1998). *Teacher preparation and selection in Pennsylvania: Ensuring high performance classroom teachers for the 21st century.* (mimeo) Pittsburgh: Heinz School of Public Policy & Management, Carnegie-Mellon University.

10. Pardington, S. "State denies a teaching crisis, except in poor school districts." *Contra Costa Times*, November 5, 2001.

11. Dezmon, B. (Ed.). (2001, January). *Minority achievement in Maryland at the millennium.* Report prepared by the Achievement Initiative for Maryland's Minority Students (AIMMS) Steering Committee. Baltimore: Maryland State Department of Education. www.msde.state.md.us/minority/pdf_files/2002/min.pdf

12. New Visions for Public Schools. (1999, February). *Crisis in leadership: Finding and keeping educational leaders for New York City's public schools.* New York: Author. www.newvisions.org/resources/report4_1.shtml.

13. Spiri, M. H. (2001, May). *School leadership and reform: Case studies of Philadelphia principals.* Occasional papers. Philadelphia: University of Pennsylvania, Consortium for Policy Research in Education. www.cpre.org/Publications/children02.pdf.

14. Rossi, R., & D. McKinney. "Why are teacher tests secret? politicians ask." *Chicago Sun-Times*, September 7, 2001. www.suntimes.com/output/news/cst-nws-main07x.html.

15. Spiri, M. H. (2001, May). *School leadership and reform: Case studies of Philadelphia principals*. Occasional papers. Philadelphia: University of Pennsylvania, Consortium for Policy Research in Education. www.cpre.org/Publications/children02.pdf.

16. Johnston, R. "System thwarts teacher's bid to transfer to needy school." *Education Week*, July 11, 2001. www.edweek.com/ew/ewstory.cfm?slug=42teacher.h20.

17. Helfand, D. "Garfield High teachers say they can deliver again." *Los Angeles Times*, July 18, 2001. www.latimes.com/news/local/la-000058754jul18.story.

18. Goodnough, A. "Strain of fourth-grade tests drives off veteran teachers." *New York Times*, June 14, 2001, p. A1; Seymour, L. "SOL tests create new dropouts: Frustrated Virginia teachers switching courses, leaving public school." *Washington Post*, July 17, 2001, p. A01.

1

THE CASE
FOR FINANCIAL INCENTIVES

Rapidly increasing student enrollments, high teacher turnover, class-size reduction initiatives, an impending wave of teacher retirements, and fewer college graduates electing to become classroom teachers have converged to create record shortages of public school teachers. This shortage is not expected to abate anytime soon, and it has sent states and local school districts scrambling to find sufficient numbers of teachers to meet demand.

A good indicator of the severity of the problem is the sheer volume of legislative activity initiated in the past few years to address teacher shortages. During the 2000 legislative session alone, legislators in 41 states introduced nearly 450 bills pertaining to teacher recruitment.[1]

Because low salaries are widely believed to be one of the chief deterrents to becoming and remaining a teacher, financial incentives have become an increasingly popular teacher recruitment and retention strategy. During 2001, 60 percent of the nation's governors considered higher pay for teachers a top priority, and legislators in 28 states introduced bills to raise teacher salaries.[2] So far, 11 states have passed legislation to increase teacher pay.[3] In addition, states and districts are offering bonuses, housing subsidies, tuition assistance, tax credits, and other monetary incentives in hopes of luring more teachers to their ranks and keeping the ones they already have.

Though a growing number of states are using financial incentives to increase their total numbers of teachers, relatively few incentives are expressly designed to channel teachers to the schools where they are needed most.[4] Only a few states have systematically developed targeted incentive programs to help districts attract qualified teachers to high-poverty, low-performing schools, despite ample evidence that these schools disproportionately employ the most underprepared and inexperienced teachers. Instead, legislators have been more favorably inclined to implement across-the-board salary increases to raise teacher salaries to the national average or to keep pace with inflation.[5] Although these approaches can help make teaching more competitive with other occupations, across-the-board pay raises do not provide the targeted incentives needed to entice sufficient numbers of well-prepared teachers to work in schools serving high concentrations of poor children.[6]

Targeted incentives are necessary because these schools continue to be the most difficult to staff, and "the difficulty of these jobs is rarely reflected in the salaries offered to teachers who fill them."[7] Schools with concentrated poverty have greater teacher and administrator shortages, fewer applications for vacancies, higher absenteeism among teachers and staff, and higher rates of teacher and administrator turnover.[8] They employ disproportionately more teachers who are uncertified, who are teaching out of field, and who are new to the school and to the profession.[9] Schools with these characteristics are invariably low-performing schools, and most teachers do not choose to work in them if they have other options.

Teachers' unions argue that lack of support from administrators and poor working conditions drive teachers from these schools. But the compensation system that determines how teachers are paid is also partly to blame. The traditional teacher salary structure bases teacher compensation solely on experience and coursework. Teacher pay generally does not differ by more rigorous preparation, higher levels of knowledge and skills, on-the-job performance, ability to teach high-demand subjects, or willingness to take on more difficult or challenging assignments. Teachers' unions have traditionally defended this salary structure as fair and objective, and they have opposed differential-pay systems that would pay some teachers more than others. But there are compelling reasons why financial incentives are essential if we are to ensure that *every* school is staffed by highly qualified teachers.

NEW REQUIREMENTS CREATE GREATER SENSE OF URGENCY

The newly reauthorized Elementary and Secondary Education Act of 2001, the *No Child Left Behind Act*, has greatly increased the pressure on school system leaders to correct staffing inequities in schools that serve large concentrations of poor and minority children. The *No Child Left Behind Act* requires that all new teachers hired with federal Title I funds after the beginning of the 2002–2003 school year must be highly qualified in the subjects they are teaching. By the end of 2005–2006, all teachers must be highly qualified, regardless of funding source. According to guidance issued by the U.S. Department of Education, this requirement applies to all public elementary and secondary school teachers who teach core academic subjects (English, reading/language arts, mathematics, science, foreign languages, civics and government, economics, arts, history, and geography). In order to meet the federal definition of "highly qualified," teachers must be fully certified by the state in which they are teaching, hold at least a bachelor's degree, and demonstrate subject matter competence in each of the core academic subjects that they teach.[10]

Furthermore, state departments of education are now required to collect information on the distribution of less-than-fully qualified teachers throughout the state and must submit a plan outlining the steps they will take to ensure that poor and minority children are not disproportionately assigned to inexperienced, uncertified, and out-of-field teachers. Districts must notify the parents of children enrolled in Title I schools that they are entitled to receive information about the qualifications of their child's teacher, and schools receiving Title I funds must notify parents if children receive instruction for four or more weeks from a teacher who is not highly qualified.[11]

Ironically, these new requirements are scheduled to take effect just as state budget shortfalls are prompting a number of states to eliminate or drastically scale back some of their incentive programs. In November 2001, for example, Virginia moved to reduce cash bonuses for accomplished teachers who achieve certification from the National Board for Professional Teaching Standards.[12] In January 2002, the Massachusetts State Department of Education announced plans to limit the number of teacher signing bonuses to be awarded during 2002 to 50, a steep drop from the 120 bonuses that had been awarded in 2000 and 2001.[13] In February 2002, the California legislature repealed $98 million that had been allocated to Teaching as a Priority grants—discretionary grants that districts had been using to provide bonuses and other incentives to recruit and retain fully certified teachers in low-performing schools.[14] Several months later, California discontinued the Governor's Teaching Fellowship Program, which had provided $20,000 fellowships to mid-career changers who enrolled in approved teacher preparation programs and committed to teach in low-performing California schools.[15] In June 2002, Massachusetts suspended its Master Teachers bonus program, eliminating the $5,000 annual bonuses that National Board Certified teachers had been eligible to receive for mentoring new teachers.[16]

Some new federal funds are available through the *No Child Left Behind Act* to help states and districts develop potential solutions—including financial incentives—to attract teachers and principals to hard-to-staff schools. Title II of the Act authorizes the appropriation of $3.175 billion in fiscal year 2002 to help states and districts prepare, train, and recruit high-quality teachers and principals. States can use Title II funds for a variety of purposes, including:

> Developing, or assisting local educational agencies in developing, merit-based performance systems, and strategies that provide differential and bonus pay for teachers in high-need academic subjects such as reading, mathematics, and science and teachers in high-poverty schools and districts.[17]

States that receive Title II grants must reserve 95 percent of the funds to make subgrants to local school districts, which can then be used in a number of different ways. Two of the approved purposes listed under Title II, Part A are:

> Developing and implementing initiatives to assist in recruiting highly qualified teachers (particularly initiatives that have proven effective in retaining highly qualified teachers), and hiring highly qualified teachers, who will be assigned teaching positions within their fields, including—
> (A) providing scholarships, signing bonuses, or other financial incentives, such as differential pay, for teachers to teach—

> (i) in academic subjects in which there exists a shortage of highly qualified teachers within a school or within the local educational agency; and
>
> (ii) in schools in which there exists a shortage of highly qualified teachers.

Developing and implementing initiatives to promote retention of highly qualified teachers and principals, particularly within elementary schools and secondary schools with a high percentage of low-achieving students, including programs that provide—

> (B) incentives, including financial incentives, to retain teachers who have a record of success in helping low-achieving students improve their academic achievement; or
>
> (C) incentives, including financial incentives, to principals who have a record of improving the academic achievement of all students, but particularly students from economically disadvantaged families, students from racial and ethnic minority groups, and students with disabilities.[18]

It is important to note that states and districts that choose to use Title II monies in these ways must link the financial rewards for teachers and principals to improved student achievement, according to guidance issued by the U.S. Department of Education:

> Because the purpose of Title II, Part A is to increase student academic achievement, programs that provide teachers and principals with merit pay, pay differential, and/or monetary bonuses should be linked to measurable increases in student academic achievement produced by the efforts of the teacher or principal.[19]

In order to design and implement financial incentives that will be most effective, school system leaders need answers to the following questions:

- What do we know about the effectiveness of using financial incentives as a policy remedy, and under what conditions are they most likely to work?
- What are the economic arguments in support of differential pay, and why have teachers' unions traditionally opposed it?
- How does teacher pay affect teacher mobility?

- Is more money likely to overcome teacher reluctance to work in hard-to-staff schools?
- What kinds of financial incentives are states, school districts, businesses, and the federal government currently offering to attract and retain teachers, especially in high-poverty, low-performing schools?
- What can we learn from incentive programs that have already been implemented?

HOW MONEY MATTERS

One of the reasons policymakers have been somewhat cautious about creating financial incentives targeted specifically to hard-to-staff schools is that they are not sure how effective differentiated-pay systems are.[20] Because most incentive programs are fairly new and limited data are available to gauge their effectiveness, this strategy is largely untested. Moreover, some argue, it is not clear whether teachers will respond in predictable ways to monetary incentives because good teachers are drawn to the profession by teaching's intrinsic rewards—in other words, "the best teachers aren't in it for the money."[21]

Yet money clearly matters. Hirsch (2001) notes that "state and regional studies aimed at supply and demand and teacher salaries suggest that teachers will cross local district and state lines for jobs and better salaries."[22] Oklahoma school districts, for example, lost approximately 1,000 teachers during the summer of 1999. According to the state department of education, the primary reason for leaving was to pursue higher pay. The majority of those who remained in teaching moved to Texas, where salaries were as much as $6,000 higher. To keep out-of-state recruiters from poaching their teachers, Oklahoma legislators raised teacher salaries $3,000 the following year.[23]

The relationship between salary and teacher supply may seem puzzling because so many of the results seem inherently contradictory. Salary plays a major role in teacher migration decisions, yet it is not the primary reason teachers enter the profession, nor is it the only reason that teachers leave the profession or switch schools. Hanushek, Kain, and Rivkin (2001), for example, found that higher salaries reduced the likelihood that teachers in Texas would leave their district, yet teacher mobility was much more strongly related to characteristics of the students than to salary. In Tennessee, teachers who had switched school districts were asked to identify the most influential factor affecting their decision to change jobs. Salary was ranked as the number one reason by the highest percentage of respondents (22 percent), but the vast majority of job changers (78 percent) said that some other factor was a greater influence on their decision than salary.[24]

How money matters becomes much clearer if salary is viewed as just one of many factors that employees weigh when assessing the relative attractiveness of any particular job, such as opportunities for advancement, difficulty of the job, physical working conditions, length of commute, flexibility of working hours, and demands on personal time. Salary matters less when other characteristics of the workplace are personally or professionally satisfying. When they are not satisfying or the work itself is significantly more demanding, salary matters more and can be the tipping point that determines whether teachers stay or leave. Adjusting salaries upward can compensate for less appealing aspects of jobs; conversely, improving the relative attractiveness of jobs can compensate for lower salaries.

Viewed in this way, it becomes clear that teachers do respond in predictable ways to monetary incentives. Results of a 2000 Public Agenda survey of beginning teachers lend support to this theory—by very high margins, new teachers "want to work in schools with involved parents, well-behaved students, smaller classes and supportive administrators, and most would even pass up significantly higher salaries in favor of working conditions that offer these."[25]

Evidence that money matters more when the job is more challenging comes from studies of staffing patterns in California and Texas school districts. Nearly half of California teachers surveyed by SRI in 2001 named pay scale and benefits as the most, second most, or third most important reason they chose the district where they work. Teachers in high-poverty, high-minority districts named pay and benefits as an important reason more often than others.[26]

Kirby, Naftel, and Berends (1999) found that minority teachers in Texas were especially sensitive to pay and working conditions, particularly those who worked in high-risk school districts where 60 percent or more of the students were economically disadvantaged. "This is not surprising," said the researchers, "given that they are working under what are likely to be rather difficult and underresourced conditions."[27] Recruiting and retaining minority teachers is a critical and urgent issue in Texas, they argue, because they disproportionately make up the teaching force in high-risk districts, which already face the most challenges and the most severe staff shortages.

Kirby et al. found that increases in pay significantly lower teacher attrition, especially among black and Hispanic teachers. A $1,000 increase in beginning teacher salaries would reduce attrition by an estimated 2.9 percent overall, and by 5–6 percent among minority teachers. In high-risk districts, a $1,000 increase in pay would reduce teacher attrition by an estimated 6.2 percent, compared to 1.6 percent in medium-risk districts and 1 percent in low-risk districts. When the researchers examined the trade-offs among several variables in terms of their effect on attrition (salary, student/teacher ratios, instructional expenditures, percentage administrative staff, percentage support staff) they found that increasing salary and lowering student/teacher ratios would have the greatest effect on teacher attrition, particularly in high-risk districts.

Weighing these two policy options, Kirby et al. sided in favor of monetary incentives:

> Lowering student/teacher ratios can be very expensive and difficult to push through the bureaucracy. Such a move can often lead to unintended consequences—witness the big increase in number of uncertified teachers in California following a mandated class-size reduction, as districts scrambled to hire more teachers to comply with that mandate. . . . Increasing teacher pay seems to hold the most promise in reducing teacher attrition, at least in terms of these results. This suggests that raising beginning teacher salaries in high-risk districts by offering signing bonuses to fully certified teachers and starting teachers who agree to teach in these districts on a higher step of the salary scale may well have an important payoff in both recruiting and retention of minority teachers.[28]

EQUITY ARGUMENTS FOR FINANCIAL INCENTIVES

Most teachers and principals do not voluntarily sign up for the toughest assignments in the poorest communities.[29] Sixty-nine percent of teachers in North Carolina, 53 percent of administrators, and 57 percent of teacher assistants polled in March 2000 said that if given the opportunity, they would not volunteer to work in a low-performing school.[30] In 2001 (when 11,000 New York City teachers, or 14 percent of the total, were uncertified), former New York City Schools Chancellor Harold Levy estimated that more than 2,000 certified teachers turned down job offers because they did not want to be assigned to one of the city's 99 lowest-performing schools.[31] Because the board of education was under court order to staff these schools with certified teachers first, recruiters actually turned away certified teachers from schools with vacancies because they were not considered failing schools. One exasperated teacher who said that she would never work in a failing school argued,

> You have to be a combination of a social worker and Mother Teresa to work in those schools. Those kids deserve a decent education, but we as teachers deserve a decent work atmosphere. We deserve to be safe. I worked so hard to get my license, I did all this schooling, and the last thing I heard, America was a country of free choice.[32]

Some New York teachers were going so far as to delay taking required state certification examinations and completing applications for teaching credentials to avoid any possibility of being assigned to one of these schools—sometimes upon the advice of school administrators. According to one principal in Queens, "The smarter people are not getting certified so they don't have to be sentenced to a SURR (Schools Under Registration Review) school."[33]

When teachers do end up in hard-to-staff, low-performing schools, they do not tend to stay in them very long. Some leave the teaching profession altogether. Some move to other school districts. And some transfer to other schools within the district, since union contracts frequently include seniority clauses that permit teachers to choose their teaching assignments as they move up the ranks. But there is a consistent and deeply disturbing pattern to the flow of teachers between schools. Recent studies conducted in Philadelphia, California, Texas, and New York show that teachers systematically move away from schools with low levels of achievement and high concentrations of poor and minority children.

In Philadelphia, for example, one-third of the jobs held by teachers in the public schools turned over between 1996 and 1999.[34] Teachers who moved didn't necessarily leave Philadelphia; migration to other schools within the district accounted for nearly half of all job changes. But when teachers did move, they tended to move to "more desirable" schools within the city (those with higher test scores, lower poverty rates, and fewer minority students).

Carroll, Reichardt, and Guarino (2000) examined teacher attrition and retention patterns in roughly 70 percent of California school districts over a three-year period.[35] They found that the odds that a teacher in California would exit a school district were positively related to the percentage of black students in the teacher's school. The relationship was significant for all teachers combined, for teachers in 4 out of 5 separate grade-level groups examined, and in both transition years included in the data (1994 to 1995 and 1995 to 1996).

When Carroll et al. examined the flow of transferring teachers within the same district, the results were dramatic. The odds that a teacher would transfer out of a particular school were positively related to both the percentage of black students and the percentage of Hispanic students in the school. Conversely, the odds that a teacher would transfer into a particular school were negatively related to both the percentages of black and the percentages of Hispanic students. In each case, the relationship was significant for all teachers combined and for every separate teacher subgroup in both of the transition years. The same general pattern was found with respect to the percentage of students in the teacher's school who were eligible for free and reduced-price lunch. Although the size of the effects varied between years and among subgroups, the researchers concluded that the pattern was clear: Teachers tend to transfer out of schools that enroll relatively high concentrations of poor and minority students and into schools with relatively low populations of poor and minority students.

Similar patterns were documented by Hanushek, Kain, and Rivkin (2001) in their three-year study of teacher mobility in Texas.[36] Between 1993 and 1996, almost 1 in 5 teaching jobs in Texas turned over each year: 14 percent of teachers left the Texas public schools, 3 percent changed school districts, and 4 percent switched schools within the same district. Contrary to conventional wisdom, Hanushek et al. found that higher salaries were not the primary reason that teachers moved from one school to another. On average, teachers who changed districts in Texas increased their earnings by only 0.4 percent.

What did change dramatically were average levels of student achievement and the proportions of poor and minority students in those districts—"strong evidence that teachers systematically favor higher-achieving, non-minority, non-low income students."[37] Average district achievement rose by 3 percentile points, while the average proportions of black, Hispanic, and poor students declined by 2.5 percent, 5 percent, and 6.6 percent, respectively, when teachers switched districts. Average district achievement and the composition of the student body changed most dramatically when teachers moved from urban to suburban districts: average achievement increased 14 percentile points, while the proportion of black, Hispanic, and poor students fell by 15–20 percent.

Even when teachers switched schools within urban districts, they tended to seek out schools with higher student achievement, fewer black and Hispanic students, and fewer students eligible for subsidized lunches. According to the researchers, "these patterns are consistent with the frequently hypothesized placement of new teachers in the most difficult teaching situations within urban districts coupled with an ability to change locations as they move up the experience ranks."[38] The only teachers who broke with this pattern were black teachers, who were more likely to move to schools with higher enrollments of black students than their originating schools. Differences in average student achievement were also much smaller for black and Hispanic teachers.

Lankford, Loeb, and Wyckoff (2002) documented similar patterns of teacher migration in New York public schools between 1993 and 1998.[39] Only 40 percent of new teachers hired in 1993 were still teaching in the same schools five years later. Those who began their teaching careers in urban schools had higher rates of teacher turnover, and those who began their teaching careers in New York City urban schools were more likely than teachers in any other area of the state to leave teaching altogether. When teachers switched districts, the average percentages of poor, minority, and limited English proficient students in their schools were cut nearly in half. The decline was even more dramatic among teachers in the New York City region who switched districts. When teachers crossed district lines, the average percentage of poor students in their schools fell from 68 percent to 21 percent, the average percentage of limited English proficient students fell from 15 percent to 6 percent, and the average percentage of nonwhite students fell from 88 percent to 40 percent. The researchers found similar trends in the transfer patterns of teachers who switched schools within the same district, but the size of the difference was much smaller.

Perhaps most important among their findings was that teachers who moved to different districts or left public teaching altogether tended to be more highly skilled than those who remained behind. Teachers who changed districts were half as likely to have failed either the General Knowledge portion of the National Teachers Examination or the New York State Liberal Arts and Science certification exam; about half as likely to hold bachelor's degrees from the least competitive colleges; and 35 percent more likely to hold bachelor's degrees from highly or most competitive colleges. Schools that had low quality teachers as measured by one attribute were more likely to have low quality teachers on other measures, and lower-performing students were more likely to be in schools with lesser-qualified teachers. Moreover, starting salaries for teachers in the New York City region who served poor, minority, and low-achieving students were considerably lower than starting salaries for other teachers in the same area—about $1,700 lower for teachers of low-performing students and about $2,800 lower for teachers of non-white and poor students. According to the researchers,

> Transfer and quit behavior of teachers is consistent with the hypothesis that more qualified teachers seize opportunities to leave difficult working conditions and move to more appealing environments. Teachers are more likely to leave poor, urban schools and those who leave are likely to have greater skills than those who stay. The current salary structure for teachers likely does not alleviate the inequitable distribution of teachers and may well make it worse.[40]

Importantly, Carroll et al., Hanushek et al., and Lankford et al. all note that it is not possible to determine from the California, Texas, and New York data whether the characteristics of the students themselves directly affected teachers' decisions to migrate, or served as proxies for other factors such as less attractive working conditions in the schools. Either way, the effect on staffing patterns was the same—experienced teachers (and in New York, the most skilled teachers) tended to shift to schools serving fewer poor, minority, and low-achieving students. This pattern strongly suggests that without intervention, schools that serve students most in need of experienced, well-prepared teachers will continue to face recurring cycles of staff vacancies. To fill these vacancies, school districts will continue to assign the most inexperienced teachers who lack the seniority to request transfers, or they will resort to filling vacancies with uncertified teachers who hold emergency permits or waivers, interns, long-term substitutes, or teachers who do not hold degrees in the subjects they are assigned to teach. These actions adversely affect school achievement and they disproportionately harm poor and minority children.

What are the alternatives? Sometimes teachers and principals can be successfully persuaded by superintendents to go where they are needed most, but this does not always work. Montgomery County, Maryland Superintendent Jerry Weast met with each of his principals in 2000 and asked the strongest to consider moving to the district's most challenging schools. Some principals agreed and voluntarily transferred to schools that had higher concentrations of poverty, greater teacher turnover, and lower test scores. But not all principals were willing to take on the additional demands and stress that these jobs inevitably entail. Others requested lesser assignments. Some eventually left the school district.[41]

Forcing teachers and principals to work in the most challenging schools is clearly not a feasible alternative, either. Even the suggestion that teachers could be asked to work in schools not of their own choosing is enough to trigger stiff opposition from teachers' unions. In California, a state task force recently recommended banning the widespread practice of assigning the least experienced teachers to the state's neediest schools.[42] The task force proposed that principals should be given the authority to determine teacher placements, instead of allowing teachers with seniority to choose their own assignments. Wayne Johnson, president of the California Teachers Association, threatened that teachers would quit rather than accept these terms:

If you think you have a teacher shortage now, wait till you do that and people know they have no right to teach where they are or where they

want to teach, that some administrator will decide where they go. . . .
They're just not going to get it done. . . . We'll see to it.[43]

New York City is another case in point. In August 2000, State Commissioner of Education Richard Mills sued the New York City Board
of Education for hiring nearly 600 uncertified teachers to staff the
city's 99 lowest-performing schools, in violation of policies adopted by
the Board of Regents in 1998.[44] Commissioner Mills ordered then-
Chancellor Harold Levy to replace the uncertified teachers in these
schools and to fill new vacancies that arose with certified teachers.
One response developed by Mr. Levy was an incentive plan to help fill
vacancies by dramatically increasing the starting salaries of experienced private and parochial school teachers who agreed to transfer
into the city's lowest-performing schools.[45] A spokesman for Commissioner Mills praised the incentive plan but suggested that Mr. Levy
should consider transferring teachers from other city schools as well,
even if they did not want to go.

Mr. Levy expressed reluctance to move teachers against their will,
noting in a memo that "historically the board has lost certified teachers
to the suburbs when it has attempted involuntarily to require new teachers to teach in undesirable locations. I view this road as folly."[46] But Mr.
Mills held firm, stating that "this court action has led to profound
changes in the way the city places teachers, and it's high time." [The failing schools] "were always last in line, and now they are first in line." He
expressed hope that teachers would reconsider working in the lowest-
performing schools where certified teachers were badly needed: "People are going to have to be guided by their better angels." Mr. Levy
countered that teachers who work in urban schools are already taking on
a substantial challenge: "People who choose urban education are doing
God's work, and where they choose to teach and how they choose to
dedicate themselves is a matter of personal reflection."[47]

Pressure from the powerful New York City teachers' union in the
form of a lawsuit or a strike added to Mr. Levy's reluctance to relocate
teachers. Randi Weingarten, president of the United Federation of
Teachers, vowed to fight involuntary transfers of experienced teachers
in court. She cautioned that "at a time when the city is begging for
teachers, you will lose people when you mandate where they work."[48]

Moreover, she warned that "forcing teachers to transfer to troubled schools would 'outrage' parents and compel the teachers to abandon New York City schools altogether."[49]

ECONOMIC ARGUMENTS FOR FINANCIAL INCENTIVES

If teachers do not choose to work in high-poverty, low-performing schools voluntarily (and *will* not work in them involuntarily), what are the alternatives? One policy option is to compensate teachers and principals at a higher rate of pay for the harder work and more difficult working conditions that these jobs entail. As economist Michael Podgursky (2001) notes,

> Differential pay by field within professions is pervasive. Cardiologists on average earn much more than general practitioners; corporate lawyers earn more than public-interest lawyers; and intensive-care nurses earn more than school nurses. Of course, there are also large differences in academic salaries by field in higher education. Even community colleges differentiate pay by field. Economists see these types of pay differentials as central to the efficient operation of markets. Professional fields that require greater training or draw on relatively specialized skills typically command higher earnings. Alternatively, some tasks involve greater stress and less pleasant working conditions. Other things being equal, these too will command higher earnings. Even the U.S. military recognizes the principle of compensating differentials with overseas and hazardous duty pay.[50]

But differential pay is not characteristic of the teaching profession. The overwhelming majority of teachers in the United States are paid according to a single-salary schedule,

> which bases pay entirely on the experience and academic credentials of teachers, [and] is a nearly universal feature of public sector teacher labor markets. Under a single-salary schedule, all of the certified teaching personnel—kindergarten as well as secondary chemistry and mathematics teachers, along with a variety of special education teachers—are paid according to the same schedule with no differentials reflecting field, individual effort, talent, or merit. By the same token, all teachers in a school

district, regardless of the character of the school's working conditions, are paid identical salaries.[51]

The problem with the single-salary schedule, economists contend, is that if all teachers in a district are compensated at the same level without regard to differences in amenities or the difficulty of the task, they will naturally tend to gravitate to jobs with less stress, fewer demands, and more desirable working conditions. In other areas of the economy, wages adjust to compensate for differences that make some jobs relatively more attractive than others. If wages are not allowed to adjust, high-poverty, low-performing schools will have much greater difficulty competing for experienced, qualified teachers. "The rigidity of the single-salary schedule," Podgursky argues,

yields perverse, unintended consequences. Rather than allowing wages to adjust to compensate for differing working conditions, teachers must adjust instead. Special education teachers "burn out" and leave the profession, or transfer over to assignments outside of special education. Troubled schools in urban districts end up with the least experienced teachers as more experienced teachers use their seniority to transfer to favored schools. Teachers move but pay doesn't.

If schools differ in terms of nonpecuniary conditions (e.g., safety, student rowdiness), then equalizing teacher pay will disequalize teacher quality. On the other hand, if districts wish to equalize quality they will need to disequalize pay. Collective bargaining agreements in large urban school districts, which impose the same salary schedule over hundreds of schools, suppress pay differentials and induce teachers to leave the most troubled schools.[52]

An additional problem with the single-salary schedule, Podgursky notes, is its disequalizing effect on spending across schools within the same district.[53] The single-salary schedule awards higher salaries to teachers with more experience, and experienced teachers tend to shift to schools serving fewer poor students. This means that districts actually spend less money per student in high-poverty schools because these schools generally employ the least experienced (and consequently the lowest paid) teachers.

Hanushek, Kain, and Rivkin (2001) conclude that higher salaries could overcome teacher reluctance to work in hard-to-staff schools, but to be effective, the increases would have to be substantial. To determine the size of the pay increase that would be required to attract and retain teachers in schools that teachers consider less desirable, Hanushek et al. estimated the effects of starting teacher salaries and various teacher and student characteristics on the probability that teachers would leave Texas school districts. By their estimates, "schools serving a high proportion of students who are academically very disadvantaged and either black or Hispanic may have to pay an additional 20, 30, or even 50 percent more in salary than those schools serving a predominantly white or Asian, academically well-prepared student body."[54] Importantly, they conclude that increases in pay must be targeted in order to work, arguing that "across the board salary increases are unlikely to compensate for the labor market disadvantages facing some schools."[55] The amount of additional compensation required to attract and retain teachers need not be as daunting, of course, if schools can improve the relative attractiveness of these jobs in other ways.

WHERE THE UNIONS STAND

Traditionally, the staunchest defenders of the single-salary schedule have been the teachers' unions themselves. According to the American Federation of Teachers, the single-salary schedule "has persisted in large part because it is viewed by teachers as equitable and by management as easy to administer."[56] One reason that teachers' unions have traditionally opposed paying some teachers more than others is that "teachers have traditionally viewed attempts to differentiate their pay as statements of the relative worth of various teaching specialties—setting off competition and fears of favoritism."[57] Merit pay systems implemented in the 1980s, which attempted to identify the "best" teachers and reward them monetarily from a limited pool of funds, were widely criticized for being arbitrary and divisive and for promoting competition among teachers rather than collaboration.[58]

The National Education Association, the nation's largest teachers' union, is adamantly opposed to some types of differential pay, such as financial incentives to recruit and retain teachers in high demand subject areas and specialties, such as mathematics, science, and bilingual education. In its 2000–2001 resolutions on salaries and other compensation, the NEA makes clear that "the Association opposes providing additional compensation to attract and/or retain education employees in hard-to-recruit positions."[59]

In some cases, local NEA affiliates have actually blocked school districts from using financial incentives to attract teachers to difficult-to-fill positions. In May 2001, for example, the Crete, Nebraska, school system was ruled to be in violation of state law because it had offered an industrial-technology teacher a $2,350 hiring bonus without first consulting the local teachers' union.[60] The school district had originally hoped to raise all beginning teachers' salaries from $21,650 to $24,000, but the proposed pay increase was rejected by the Crete Education Association. As a result of the new ruling, the district was prohibited from providing the bonus to the teacher the following year, and other small districts across the state were obliged to withdraw bonus offers they had made to new recruits in order to compete with larger school districts for teachers.

In Missouri, another small school district is being sued by the local teachers' union for offering signing bonuses to recruit teachers in shortage areas. In 2001, the Sherwood Cass School District offered $1,000 to $2,000 bonuses to seven teachers with specializations in physics, chemistry, special education, and other hard-to-staff subject areas.[61] Although both the Missouri State Teachers Association and the Missouri School Boards' Association supported the school district's use of bonuses as a recruiting tool, the Sherwood NEA claimed that the extra pay violated the district teachers' contract and the Missouri Teacher Tenure Act, which requires districts to adopt uniform salary schedules.

Although the NEA opposes differential pay for hard-to-recruit subject area positions, it is important to note that the NEA *supports* differential pay to attract and retain teachers in low-performing schools. This critical distinction was clarified in a December 6, 2000, internal memorandum on NEA policies regarding teacher compensation systems. According to this memorandum,

NEA supports the use of financial incentives—in appropriate circumstances as determined locally—to encourage teachers with the requisite qualifications—particularly those who already are employed in the school district—to accept employment in low-performing schools. Care should be taken in designing and implementing a compensation system of this type not to solve the problem of low-performing schools in one school district by attracting teachers from such schools in other districts—thereby exacerbating the problem in the latter school districts.[62]

In fact, higher pay in low-performing or hard-to-staff schools has wide appeal among teachers. In April 2000, when Public Agenda surveyed public school teachers who had been in the field for five years or less, the overwhelming majority (84 percent) said they believed that it was a good idea to pay higher salaries to teachers "who agree to work in difficult schools with hard-to-educate children."[63]

In March 2000, NEA's North Carolina affiliate found that even though the majority of North Carolina teachers, administrators, and teacher assistants said that they would not volunteer to work in a low-performing school, more than 75 percent said they would consider it if a signing bonus were offered.[64] The same month, the president of NEA's New York affiliate made the following statement of support for financial incentives in a press release entitled *NEA/NY Applauds Senate Plan to Improve Teacher Quality*:

> NEA/NY is encouraged by the Senate plan to provide $3,400 in cash grants to teachers who commit to teach for four years in areas where a shortage is greatest, financial incentives to recruit retired teachers back to the classroom, and the $10,000 salary bonuses for experienced teachers who agree to teach in low-performing schools for three years.[65]

The American Federation of Teachers, the nation's second-largest teachers' union, is also willing to consider alternative pay strategies to attract and retain teachers in low-performing and hard-to-staff schools. In February 2001, the AFT adopted a resolution on professional compensation for teachers that acknowledged "increased compensation is necessary to attract teachers to difficult assignments and shortage areas if we are to have qualified teachers in every classroom."[66] This landmark resolution says that the AFT is "encouraging its locals to explore various teacher compensation systems based on local conditions," but makes clear that AFT is recommending enhancing and improving, not abandoning, the traditional salary structure. According to the AFT,

A professional teacher compensation system could include financial incentives to teachers who acquire additional knowledge and skill; advanc-
ing skills such as National Board for Professional Teaching Standards certification; or who agree to teach in low-performing and hard-to-staff
schools. The AFT believes that compensation proposals could include increased pay for schoolwide improvement, mentoring new and veteran
teachers and teaching in shortage areas.[67]

The AFT and many others also point out, however, that money alone
is not sufficient to attract and keep good teachers. Recruiting bonuses
and other financial incentives may help attract more teachers initially,
but they are not likely to work in the long run unless they are accom-
panied by good-faith efforts to improve working conditions and give
teachers the specialized preparation needed to succeed in the nation's
most challenging classrooms.[68] Few teachers will be swayed by financial incentives if they suspect that they are purely compensatory measures to make up for bad working conditions, lack of resources, and
poor leadership, rather than part of a larger plan to make teaching in
hard-to-staff schools personally and professionally rewarding.[69] As
Harvard education professor Richard Murnane points out, "Paying
people extra money to do an impossible job doesn't work, and you
need to make the jobs doable such that at the end of the day, people
feel glad that they're there."[70]

Clearly, there are ways that school system leaders can make these jobs
more doable, by reallocating resources to the schools that serve students
with the greatest needs, improving school leadership, reducing class
size, increasing professional development, clamping down on student
discipline problems, improving school safety, creating strong induction
programs to support beginning teachers, and giving teachers more authority. But it is unrealistic to expect that school districts can solve this
problem alone. Limited resources and external political pressures can
impede progress, and other factors that make certain schools less desirable remain largely outside of a school's control, such as its location, the
safety of the surrounding neighborhood, and the greater non-academic
health and social needs of poor children. The fact remains that "hard-to-
staff schools serve children with more special needs and fewer social advantages, and teachers are not compensated for gaining the special skills

necessary to meet these students' greater needs."[71] All indicators suggest that paying teachers more money to take on jobs that are substantially harder is an essential part of the solution.

One of the strongest advocates for this position turns out to be New York City's United Federation of Teachers. Though they remain adamantly opposed to any plan that would involuntarily transfer teachers to low-performing schools, the union favors monetary incentives to attract teachers to these schools voluntarily. In fact, when Commissioner Mills sued the Board of Education in 2000, the UFT proposed that the city expand an incentive program that former Chancellor Rudy Crew had implemented in 39 of the 99 Schools Under Registration Review. Certified teachers who agreed to transfer into the 39 schools received a 15 percent pay raise in exchange for working 40 extra minutes per day and participating in an extra week of training at the beginning of the school year. The incentive prompted about 600 teachers to apply for transfers to these schools, about half of whom were accepted. The union argued that the extra training teachers in these schools received paid off in terms of higher student achievement, too, noting that the percentage of 4th and 8th graders who passed standardized achievement tests in reading increased by 7.1 percent in the "extended-time" SURR schools, compared to 3.4 percent in the other SURR schools.

UFT president Randi Weingarten claimed that if the incentive were expanded to all 99 SURR schools, the city could fill every job opening with certified teachers.[72] According to Ms. Weingarten, "We are offering to the court and to the parties what we believe will be a very innovative and effective solution. . . . We believe this will not only help solve the problem of getting seasoned, certified teachers into these other SURR schools, but it will give thousands of other kids a better chance to succeed." The proposal, estimated to cost $30 million to $60 million, required the approval of then-Mayor Rudolph Giuliani, who controlled the school system's budget. An aide to Mr. Levy said that the Chancellor's office was considering every option, but then-Deputy Mayor Anthony Coles suggested that "there are also a number of other initiatives that can help turn around failing schools," such as privatization and merit pay, which the teachers' union opposes.

It is highly likely that critics will continue to press for alternatives such as privatization and vouchers to solve the persistent problem of staffing low-performing schools. The Bush Administration, for example, has proposed spending $3.7 billion over five years on a federal income tax credit to enable parents to withdraw their children from low-performing public schools.[73] Rather than using the money to improve these schools by increasing teacher compensation and improving working conditions so that teachers will not want to leave, the proposal will allow parents to claim up to $2,500 per year toward the costs of tuition, fees, and transportation so that they can remove their children from public schools identified as failing under new federal guidelines.

It is increasingly clear that school system leaders and teachers' unions must come to terms with what it will take to attract and retain qualified teachers in the most challenging schools or run the risk of losing all credibility in the fight against vouchers. As Miller (1999) points out, "increasing numbers of urban parents… want a way out. It seems immoral to argue that they must wait for the day when urban public schools are somehow 'fixed.' It's even harder to argue that bigger voucher programs could make things worse."[74]

The NEA, the AFT, and New York City's United Federation of Teachers, in particular, have indicated that they are willing to consider alternatives to the traditional teacher salary schedule as a potential solution. Equally encouraging is a growing interest among policymakers in financial incentives as a market-based policy remedy. The next chapter reviews the kinds of financial incentives that states, districts, businesses, and the federal government are currently offering to attract and retain quality educators, especially in high-poverty, low-performing schools.

NOTES

1. Hirsch, E. (2001, February). *Teacher recruitment: Staffing classrooms with quality teachers*, p. 13. Denver: State Higher Education Executive Officers. www.sheeo.org/quality/mobility/recruitment.pdf.

2. Blair, J. "Lawmakers plunge into teacher pay." *Education Week*, February 21, 2001. www.edweek.com/ew/ewstory.cfm?slug=23salary.h20

3. Hirsch, E. (2001, February). *Teacher recruitment: Staffing classrooms with quality teachers*, p. 7. Denver: State Higher Education Executive Officers. www.sheeo.org/quality/mobility/recruitment.pdf.

4. Olson, L. "Sweetening the pot." In *Education Week*. (2000, January). "Quality Counts 2000: Who should teach?" www.edweek.com/sreports/qc00/templates/article.cfm?slug=recruit.htm.

5. Blair, J. "Lawmakers plunge into teacher pay." *Education Week*, February 21, 2001. www.edweek.com/ew/ewstory.cfm?slug=23salary.h20.

6. Hanushek, E. A., J. F. Kain, & S. G. Rivkin. (2001, November). *Why public schools lose teachers*. Working Paper 8599. Cambridge, MA: National Bureau of Economic Research. www.nber.org/papers/w8599; Lankford, H., S. Loeb, & J. Wyckoff. (2002, Spring). Teacher sorting and the plight of urban schools: A descriptive analysis. *Educational Evaluation and Policy Analysis, 24*(1), 37–62; Hassel, B. (2002, May). *Better pay for better teaching: Making teacher compensation pay off in the age of accountability*. Washington, D.C.: Progressive Policy Institute. www.ndol.org/documents/Hassel_May02.pdf.

7. Shields, P. M., et al. (1999). *The status of the teaching profession: Research findings and policy recommendations. A report to the Teaching and California's Future Task Force*. Santa Cruz, CA: The Center for the Future of Teaching and Learning. www.cftl.org/publications.html.

8. Lee, J. (1998). Teacher staffing and distribution patterns for 1997 in four Maryland LEAs. Paper presented at The Harvard Conference on Civil Rights and High Stakes K–12 Testing, December 4, 1998, New York. In Dezmon, B. (Ed.). (2001, January). *Minority achievement in Maryland at the millennium*. Report prepared by the Achievement Initiative for Maryland's Minority Students (AIMMS) Steering Committee. Baltimore: Maryland State Department of Education; www.msde.state.md.us/minority/pdf-files/2002/min.pdf New Visions for Public Schools. (1999, February). *Crisis in leadership: Finding and keeping educational leaders for New York City's public schools*. New York: Author. www.newvisions.org/resources/report4_1.shtml; Lippman, L., S. Burns, & E. McArthur. (1996, June). *Urban schools: The challenge of location and poverty*. NCES 96–184. Washington, D.C.: U.S. Department of Education, National Center for Education Statistics. www.nces.ed.gov/pubs/96184all.pdf, Bruno, J. E. (2002, July 26). The geographical distribution of teacher absenteeism in large urban school district settings: Implications for school reform efforts aimed at promoting equity and excellence in education. *Education Policy Analysis Archives, 10*(32). epaa.asu.edu/epaa/v10n32; Lankford, H., S. Loeb, & J. Wyckoff (2002, Spring). Teacher sorting and the plight of urban schools: A descriptive analysis. *Educational Evaluation and Policy Analysis, 24*(1), 37–62; Viadero, D. "Philadelphia study: Teacher transfers add to educational inequities." *Education Week*, April 18, 2001. www.edweek.com/ew/ewstory.cfm?slug=31Mobility.h20; Watson, S. (2001, May). *Recruiting and retaining teachers: Keys to improving the Philadelphia Public Schools*. Philadelphia:

University of Pennsylvania, Consortium for Policy Research in Education. www.cpre.org/Publications/children01.pdf; Carroll, S., R. Reichardt, & C. Guarino. (2000, October). *The distribution of teachers among California's school districts and schools.* MR-1298.0-JIF. Santa Monica, CA: RAND; Hanushek, E.A., J. F. Kain, & S. G. Rivkin (2001, November). *Why public schools lose teachers,* p. 12. Working Paper 8599. Cambridge, MA: National Bureau of Economic Research. www.nber.org/papers/w8599; Prince, C. (2002, January). *The challenge of attracting good teachers and principals to struggling schools.* Arlington, VA: American Association of School Administrators. www.aasa.org/issues_and_ insights/issues_dept/challenges.htm.

9. Maryland State Education That Is Multicultural Advisory Council. (1998, September). *Minority achievement in Maryland: The state of the state.* Baltimore: Maryland State Department of Education. www.msde.state.md.us/ minority/pdf_files/minority.pdf; Lee, J. (1998). Teacher staffing and distribution patterns for 1997 in four Maryland LEAs. Paper presented at The Harvard Conference on Civil Rights and High Stakes K–12 Testing, December 4, 1998, New York. In Dezmon, B. (Ed.). (2001, January). *Minority achievement in Maryland at the millennium.* Report prepared by the Achievement Initiative for Maryland's Minority Students (AIMMS) Steering Committee. Baltimore: Maryland State Department of Education. www.msde.state.md.us/minority/ pdf_files/2002/min.pdf; Watson, S. (2001, May). *Recruiting and retaining teachers: Keys to improving the Philadelphia Public Schools.* Philadelphia: University of Pennsylvania, Consortium for Policy Research in Education. www.cpre.org/Publications/children01.pdf; Useem, B. *In middle schools, teacher shortage reaches crisis levels.* www.philaedfund.org/notebook/ Teacher%20Shortage.htm; The Center for the Future of Teaching and Learning. (2000). *Teaching and California's future: The status of the teaching profession 2000. An update to the Teaching and California's Future Task Force, summary report.* Santa Cruz, CA: Author. www.cftl.org/documents/2000summary_ report.pdf; Rossi, R., B. Beaupre, & K. Grossman. "5,243 Illinois teachers failed key exams." *Chicago Sun-Times,* September 6, 2001. www.suntimes.com/ output/news/cst-nws-main06.html; Grossman, K., B. Beaupre, & R. Rossi. "Poorest kids often wind up with the weakest teachers." *Chicago Sun-Times,* September 7, 2001. www.suntimes.com/output/news/cst-nws-main07.html; Rossi, R. "Teacher woes worst in poor schools." *Chicago Sun-Times,* October 10, 2001. www.suntimes.com/output/news/cst-nws-teach10.html; Ingersoll, R. (2001, January). *Teacher turnover, teacher shortages, and the organization of schools.* Seattle: University of Washington, Center for the Study of Teaching and Policy. www.depts.washington.edu/ctpmail/PDFs/Turnover-Ing-01-2001.pdf; Haycock, K. (1998, Summer). Good teaching matters: How well-

qualified teachers can close the gap. *Thinking K–16*, 3(2), 1–14. Washington, D.C.: The Education Trust; Lankford, H., S. Loeb, & J. Wyckoff. (2002, Spring). Teacher sorting and the plight of urban schools: A descriptive analysis. *Educational Evaluation and Policy Analysis*, 24(1), 37–62.

10. U.S. Department of Education. (2002, June 6). *Improving Teacher Quality state grants: Title II, Part A, non-regulatory draft guidance*, p. 31. www.ed.gov/offices/OESE/SIP/TitleIIguidance2002.doc.

11. Hill, T. L. (2002). *No Child Left Behind policy brief: Teaching quality*, p. 3. Denver: Education Commission of the States. www.ecs.org/clearinghouse/34/63/3463.pdf.

12. Mathews, J. "Virginia to trim teacher bonuses." *Washington Post*, November 20, 2001, p. B07.

13. Hayward, E. "Applications for teacher signing bonus drop." *Boston Herald*, January 30, 2002. www2.bostonherald.com/news/local_regional/mint01302002.htm.

14. Sack, J. L. "Revenue shortfall prompts big school cuts in California." *Education Week*, February 6, 2002. www.edweek.com/ew/newstory.cfm?slug=21calif.h21.

15. CalTeach. "Incentive programs for teachers in low-performing schools." www.calteach.com/rewards/in3.cfm?t=3.

16. Massachusetts Department of Education. "Immediate changes to National Board program and Master Teacher program." Memorandum from David P. Driscoll, Commissioner of Education, to National Board certified teachers and candidates, June 12, 2002. www.doe.mass.edu/news/news.asp?id=772; Massachusetts Department of Education. "Poor economy forces suspension of Master Teacher bonus program." Press release, June 13, 2002. www.doe.mass.edu/news/news.asp?id=771; Hayward, E. "Mass. teachers decry demise of mentor program, stipends." *Boston Herald*, June 14, 2002. www2.bostonherald.com/news/local_regional/teac06142002.htm.

17. Public Law 107-110, the *No Child Left Behind Act of 2001* [H.R. 1], Title II, Part A, Subpart 1, Section 2113(c)(12). www.ed.gov/legislation/ESEA02/pg21.html.

18. Public Law 107-110, the *No Child Left Behind Act of 2001* [H.R. 1], Title II, Part A, Subpart 2, Sections 2123(a)(2)(A); 2123(a)(4)(C); and 2123(a)(4)(D). www.ed.gov/legislation/ESEA02/pg22.html#sec2123.

19. U.S. Department of Education. (2002, June 6). *Improving Teacher Quality state grants: Title II, Part A, non-regulatory draft guidance*, p. 31. www.ed.gov/offices/OESE/SIP/TitleIIguidance2002.doc.

20. Blair, J. "Lawmakers plunge into teacher pay." *Education Week*, February 21, 2001. www.edweek.com/ew/ewstory.cfm?slug=23salary.h20.

21. Mathews, J. "The smart money: In an effort to improve struggling schools officials increasingly use financial bonuses to lure good teachers." *Washington Post*, April 10, 2001, p. A12.

22. Hirsch, E. (2001, February). *Teacher recruitment: Staffing classrooms with quality teachers*, p. 12. Denver: State Higher Education Executive Officers. www.sheeo.org/quality/mobility/recruitment.pdf.

23. Blair, J. "Districts wooing teachers with bonuses, incentives." *Education Week*, August 2, 2000. www.edweek.com/ew/ewstory.cfm?slug=43raid.h19

24. Tennessee Advisory Commission on Intergovernmental Relations. (2000, February). "Teacher mobility among Tennessee school districts: A survey of causes." *TACIR Staff Research Briefs*, 6. www.state.tn.us/tacir/PDF_FILES/Education/Migration.pdf.

25. Farkas, S., J. Johnson, & T. Foleno, with A. Duffett, & P. Foley. (2000). *A sense of calling: Who teaches and why*. New York: Public Agenda. Summary available online. www.publicagenda.org/specials/teachers/teachers.htm.

26. Shields, P. M., et al. (1999). *The status of the teaching profession: Research findings and policy recommendations. A report to the Teaching and California's Future Task Force*, p. 49. Santa Cruz, CA: The Center for the Future of Teaching and Learning. www.cftl.org/publications.html.

27. Kirby, S. N., S. Naftel, & M. Berends. (1999). *Staffing at-risk school districts in Texas: Problems and prospects*, pp. 57–58. Santa Monica, CA: RAND. www.rand.org/publications/MR/MR1083/.

28. Kirby, S. N., S. Naftel, & M. Berends. (1999). *Staffing at-risk school districts in Texas: Problems and prospects*, p. 66. Santa Monica, CA: RAND. www.rand.org/publications/MR/MR1083/.

29. Southeast Center for Teaching Quality. (2002, January). *Recruiting teachers for hard-to-staff schools: Solutions for the Southeast and the nation*, p. 5. Chapel Hill, NC: Author. www.teachingquality.org/resources/pdfs/hard_to_staff_schools_regional_brief.pdf.

30. North Carolina Association of Educators. (2000, July). *Getting it right: Improving the ABC's of North Carolina*. ABC Survey Result Summary. www.ncae.org/news/abcsurvey/abcsurvey.shtml

31. Grace, M. "Teachers ducking certificates: Fear being assigned to bad schools." *New York Daily News*, April 24, 2001. www.nydailynews.com/2001-04-24/News_and_Views/City_Beat/a-108498.asp; Gittrich, G. "The certification disincentive: 'Reward' is often job at bad school." *New York Daily News*, April 24, 2001. www.nydailynews.com/2001-04-24/News_and_Views/City_Beat/a-108495.asp.

32. Goodnough, A., & T. Kelley. "Newly certified teachers, looking for a job, find a paradox." *New York Times*, September 1, 2000.

33. Grace, M. "Teachers ducking certificates: Fear being assigned to bad schools." *New York Daily News*, April 24, 2001. www.nydailynews. com/2001-04-24/News_and_Views/City_Beat/a-108498.asp; Gittrich, G. "The certification disincentive: 'Reward' is often job at bad school." *New York Daily News*, April 24, 2001. www.nydailynews.com/2001-04-24/ News_and_Views/City_Beat/a-108495.asp.

34. Viadero, D. "Philadelphia study: Teacher transfers add to educational inequities." *Education Week*, April 18, 2001. www.edweek.com/ew/ewstory .cfm?slug=31Mobility.h20.

35. Carroll, S., R. Reichardt, & C. Guarino. (2000, October). *The distribution of teachers among California's school districts and schools*. MR-1298.0-JIF. Santa Monica, CA: RAND.

36. Hanushek, E. A., J. F. Kain, & S. G. Rivkin. (2001, November). *Why public schools lose teachers*. Working Paper 8599. Cambridge, MA: National Bureau of Economic Research. www.nber.org/papers/w8599.

37. Hanushek, E. A., J. F. Kain, & S. G. Rivkin. (2001, November). *Why public schools lose teachers*, p. 12. Working Paper 8599. Cambridge, MA: National Bureau of Economic Research. www.nber.org/papers/w8599.

38. Hanushek, E. A., J. F. Kain, & S. G. Rivkin. (2001, November). *Why public schools lose teachers*, p. 13. Working Paper 8599. Cambridge, MA: National Bureau of Economic Research. www.nber.org/papers/w8599.

39. Lankford, H., S. Loeb, & J. Wyckoff. (2002, Spring). Teacher sorting and the plight of urban schools: A descriptive analysis. *Educational Evaluation and Policy Analysis*, 24(1), 37–62.

40. *Ibid*, p. 55.

41. Nakamura, D., & C. A. Samuels. "In school, changes at the top: Area faces shortage of new principals." *Washington Post*, June 25, 2000, p. A01.

42. Professional Development Task Force. (2001). *Learning . . . Teaching . . . Leading . . . : The Report of the Professional Development Task Force*. Sacramento: California Department of Education. http://goldmine.cde.ca.gov/ cdepress/learnteachlead.pdf.

43. Pardington, S. "State education study irks unions." *Contra Costa Times*, October 23, 2001.

44. Goodnough, A. "Political memo: Levy is sparring with an old ally over direction of the City schools." *New York Times*, August 10, 2000.

45. Goodnough, A. "Levy offers higher salaries to staff the worst schools." *New York Times*, August 2, 2000. www.nytimes.com/library/national/regional/ 080200ny-levy-edu.html.

46. Goodnough, A. "Political memo: Levy is sparring with an old ally over direction of the City schools." *New York Times*, August 10, 2000.

47. Goodnough, A., & T. Kelley. "Newly certified teachers, looking for a job, find a paradox." *New York Times*, September 1, 2000.

48. Goodnough, A., & T. Kelley. "Newly certified teachers, looking for a job, find a paradox." *New York Times*, September 1, 2000.

49. Goodnough, A. "Levy offers higher salaries to staff the worst schools." *New York Times*, August 2, 2000. www.nytimes.com/library/national/regional/080200ny-levy-edu.html.

50. Podgursky, M. (2001). "Regulation versus markets: The case for greater flexibility in the market for public school teachers," p. 137. *In* Wang, M. C., & H. J. Walberg. (Eds.). *Tomorrow's Teachers,* pp. 117–148. Richmond, CA: McCutchan Publishing Corporation.

51. Podgursky, M. (2001). "Regulation versus markets: The case for greater flexibility in the market for public school teachers," p. 135. *In* Wang, M. C., & H. J. Walberg (Eds.). *Tomorrow's Teachers*, pp. 117–148. Richmond, CA: McCutchan Publishing Corporation.

52. Podgursky, M. (2001). "Regulation versus markets: The case for greater flexibility in the market for public school teachers," pp. 137–138. *In* Wang, M. C., & H. J. Walberg (Eds.). *Tomorrow's Teachers*, pp. 117–148. Richmond, CA: McCutchan Publishing Corporation.

53. Personal communication, Michael Podgursky, July 18, 2002.

54. Hanushek, E. A., J. F. Kain, & S. G. Rivkin. (2001, November). *Why public schools lose teachers*, p. 19. Working Paper 8599. Cambridge, MA: National Bureau of Economic Research. www.nber.org/papers/w8599.

55. Hanushek, E. A., J. F. Kain, & S. G. Rivkin. (2001, November). *Why public schools lose teachers*, p. 19. Working Paper 8599. Cambridge, MA: National Bureau of Economic Research. www.nber.org/papers/w8599.

56. American Federation of Teachers. *AFT on the issues: Merit pay, "pay-for-performance," and professional teacher compensation.* www.aft.org/issues/meritpay/meritpay.html.

57. Bradley, A. "High-tech field luring teachers from education." *Education Week*, January 19, 2000. www.edweek.com/ew/ewstory.cfm?slug=19gap.h19.

58. Odden, A., C. Kelley, H. Heneman, & A. Milanowski. (2001, November). "Enhancing teacher quality through knowledge- and skills-based pay." *CPRE Policy Briefs*, RB-34. Philadelphia: University of Pennsylvania, Consortium for Policy Research in Education. www.cpre.org/Publications/rb34.pdf.

59. National Education Association. *NEA 2000–2001 Resolutions: F-9. Salaries and Other Compensation.* www.nea.org/resolutions/00/00f-9.html.

60. Reid, K. S. "News in brief: A state capitals roundup. Hiring bonuses shot down in Neb." *Education Week*, June 6, 2001. www.edweek.com/ew/ewstory .cfm?slug=39caps.h20.

61. Associated Press. "Union sues over extra pay aimed at recruiting teachers." *St. Louis Post-Dispatch*, June 2, 2002.

62. National Education Association. Internal memorandum, December 6, 2000.

63. Farkas, S., J. Johnson, & T. Foleno, with A. Duffett, & P. Foley. (2000). *A sense of calling: Who teaches and why.* New York: Public Agenda. Summary available online. www.publicagenda.org/specials/teachers/teachers.htm.

64. North Carolina Association of Educators. (2000, July). *Getting it right: Improving the ABC's of North Carolina.* ABC Survey Result Summary. www .ncae.org/news/abcsurvey/abcsurvey.shtml.

65. NEA/NY (National Education Association, New York Affiliate). "NEA/NY applauds Senate plan to improve teacher quality." Press release, March 7, 2000. Statement by Gregory S. Nash, President, National Education Association of New York, NEA/NY. www.neany.org/pressrelease/030700.html.

66. Archer, J. "AFT to urge locals to consider new pay strategies." *Education Week*, February 21, 2001. www.edweek.com/ew/ewstory.cfm?slug=23aft.h20; American Federation of Teachers. *AFT on the issues: Merit pay, "pay-for-performance," and professional teacher compensation.* www.aft.org/issues/ meritpay/meritpay.html.

67. American Federation of Teachers. *AFT on the issues: Merit pay, "pay-for-performance," and professional teacher compensation.* www.aft.org/issues/ meritpay/meritpay.html.

68. Southeast Center for Teaching Quality. (2002, January). *Recruiting teachers for hard-to-staff schools: Solutions for the Southeast and the nation,* p. 5. Chapel Hill, NC: Author. www.teachingquality.org/resources/pdfs/hard_ to_staff_schools_regional_brief.pdf.

69. Claycomb, C. (2000, Winter). High-quality urban school teachers: What they need to enter and to remain in hard-to-staff schools. *The State Education Standard,* 17–20. www.nasbe.org/Educational_Issues/Articles/1_ Winter2000/Claycomb%20article.pdf.

70. Viadero, D. "Study: Teachers seek better working conditions." *Education Week*, January 9, 2002. www.edweek.com/ew/newstory.cfm?slug=16pay.h21.

71. Southeast Center for Teaching Quality. (2002, January). *Recruiting teachers for hard-to-staff schools: Solutions for the Southeast and the nation,* p. 5. Chapel Hill, NC: Author. www.teachingquality.org/resources/pdfs/hard_ to_staff_schools_regional_brief.pdf.

72. Goodnough, A. "Union seeks more incentives to staff troubled schools." *New York Times*, August 12, 2000.

73. Robelen, E. W., & M. Walsh. "Bush proposal: Give tax credit for K–12 tuition." *Education Week*, February 13, 2002. www.edweek.com/ew/newstory .cfm?slug=22choice.h21.

74. Miller, M. "A bold experiment to fix city schools." *The Atlantic,* July 1999. www.theatlantic.com/issues/99jul/9907vouchers.htm.

2

TYPES OF FINANCIAL INCENTIVES

Financial incentives can be designed to increase the pool of qualified teachers in 3 ways. First, they can attract more people into the teaching profession by encouraging college students to choose teaching as a career, or by creating alternative routes for mid-career professionals. Second, they can reduce attrition among those already in the teaching force by enhancing compensation, or by enabling paraprofessionals and teachers who hold a variety of temporary and emergency credentials to become fully certified teachers. Third, they can draw from the reserve pool by enticing credentialed teachers who have stepped out to reenter the profession, or by encouraging retired teachers to return to the classroom without loss of pension benefits.

Although the number and variety of financial incentives to recruit and retain teachers has mushroomed in the last several years, relatively few states have systematically developed incentives that are focused and powerful enough to motivate a sufficient supply of teachers to serve in low-performing and hard-to-staff schools. As Virginia Roach, deputy executive director for the National Association of State Boards of Education points out, "One of the biggest issues are blanket state policies that aren't refined enough to meet the real needs of the state. They basically just pump out more teachers."[1] Two states that are exceptions are New York and California.

New York's Teachers of Tomorrow program was created in 2000 to "assist school districts in the recruitment, retention and certification activities necessary to increase the supply of qualified teachers in school districts experiencing a teacher shortage, especially those with low-performing schools."[2] In 2000 and 2001, the Teachers of Tomorrow program provided $25 million to fund activities in 6 categories:

1. Teacher recruitment incentives: Provides annual $3,400 bonuses to teachers willing to teach in a designated teacher shortage area or subject shortage area. Teachers are eligible to receive the bonuses for up to 4 years.
2. Certification stipends: Provides up to $2,000 for test preparation workshops or coursework leading to initial or provisional certification; reserved for teachers with temporary certificates who agree to teach for at least 1 year in a designated teacher shortage area or subject shortage area.
3. Summer in the City internship program: Provides stipends of up to $2,000 to teacher candidates who complete internships in urban schools in New York City, Buffalo, Rochester, Syracuse, and Yonkers. Participating students may use a portion of the funds for housing costs and may receive college credit and credit for field experience.
4. New York State Master Teacher program: Provides annual bonuses of $10,000 to teachers certified by the National Board for Professional Teaching Standards who agree to serve in low-performing public schools. Teachers are eligible to receive the bonuses for up to 3 years.
5. Teacher recruitment tuition reimbursement program: Provides up to $2,100 to reimburse the cost of coursework required to earn permanent or professional certification; reserved for teachers with initial or provisional certification who agree to teach for 1 year in a designated teacher shortage area or subject shortage area. The stipend may be renewed 1 additional year.
6. Summer teacher training program: Provides an intensive summer training course for teachers employed for the first time in New York City public schools; reserved for teachers who agree to teach for at least 1 year in a designated teacher shortage area or subject shortage area.

California has developed even more incentives, allocating more than $300 million to teacher recruitment and retention initiatives between 2000 and 2001.[3] These initiatives have been credited with helping increase the quantity and quality of the state's teacher pool over the past few years. Between 2000 and 2002, for example, the state reduced the number of emergency credentialed teachers by 4,000.[4] Some of California's incentives are available to all credentialed teachers, such as:

1. Loan forgiveness: State assumes up to $11,000 in student loan payments to lenders if teacher candidates agree to teach in California public schools for at least 4 years.
2. Tax credits: Allows credentialed teachers with at least 4 years of service who are actively teaching to claim annual state income tax credits ranging from $150 to $2,500, depending on the number of years of teaching service.
3. Professional development stipends: Awards stipends of $1,000 to $2,000 to credentialed teachers participating in Professional Development Institute programs.
4. Additional retirement benefits: Provides a tax-deferred annuity that allows members of the California State Teachers Retirement System to increase their contributions to a supplemental retirement account that can result in thousands of dollars of additional benefits to teachers upon retirement.
5. Bonuses for National Board Certified Teachers: Awards one-time bonuses of $10,000 to accomplished teachers who achieve certification from the National Board for Professional Teaching Standards.

Additional benefits and incentives targeted specifically to California teachers who agree to serve in low-performing schools include:

1. Loan forgiveness: Assumes up to $19,000 in student loan payments to lenders if teacher candidates agree to teach in low-performing California public schools for at least 4 years and teach in a subject shortage area.
2. Housing incentives: Allows cities and counties to use tax credits or mortgage revenue bonds to reduce the federal income tax liability

or mortgage interest rates of teachers who commit to serve at least 5 years in a low-performing school.

3. Additional bonuses for National Board Certified Teachers: Awards a supplemental $20,000 bonus to National Board Certified Teachers who serve in low-performing schools for 4 years, in addition to the one-time $10,000 bonus that all National Board Certified Teachers in California receive.

Until recently, college graduates who wished to become teachers in California were also eligible for $20,000 fellowships through the Governor's Teaching Fellowship Program.[5] Teaching Fellows were required to enroll full-time in an approved teacher preparation program and commit to teach in low-performing California schools.[6] The number of Governor's Fellowships awarded quadrupled in one year, from 250 during the 2000–2001 school year to 1,000 during 2001–2002.[7] However, this program has been discontinued.

Budget cuts have also forced California to discontinue Teaching as a Priority (TAP) block grants that school districts had been using to attract and retain credentialed teachers in low-performing schools. In 2000–2001, the state legislature allocated $118.6 million to the TAP block grant program, which districts used to offer signing bonuses, increase teacher compensation, and improve working conditions.[8] Anaheim, for example, used its allotment of $800,000 to award $2,500 signing bonuses to each new, fully credentialed teacher willing to work in one of 23 low-performing schools, and an additional $2,000 if he or she remained in the school a second year. The district also offered up to $19,000 in student loan forgiveness, relocation loans to teachers moving into the state or the county, and finder's fees to school district employees who referred fully certified teachers. According to district officials, vacancies in the school district fell from 120 in July of 1999, to 0 in 2001, allowing the district to begin the 2001–2002 school year with all teachers fully certified for the first time in at least 5 years.[9]

Though no other states come close to matching the array of financial incentives that New York and California have implemented, growing numbers of states and districts (and in some cases, corporations and the federal government) are experimenting with salary increases, bonuses, housing subsidies, tuition assistance, tax incentives, and other monetary incentives to increase teacher supply and retention. Examples of teacher incentives developed in each of these areas follow.

TARGETED SALARY INCREASES FOR HARD-TO-RECRUIT POSITIONS

Eleven states have increased teacher pay since 2000—Alabama, Arkansas, California, Connecticut, Iowa, Louisiana, Michigan, North Carolina, Oklahoma, Texas, and West Virginia. Some have instituted across-the-board pay raises to increase salaries for all teachers, while others have targeted salary increases to beginning teachers, since teacher turnover is highest during the first few years of teaching.

Because the traditional salary schedule generally prohibits districts from offering higher salaries to teachers who teach certain subjects or work in certain schools, some districts are circumventing the problem by starting high-demand teachers at higher steps on the salary ladder, a practice that the AFT currently supports.[10] In 2000, for example, the Boston teachers' union contract allowed the district to hire teachers in high-demand subject areas at the top of the pay scale, at nearly $56,000 per year rather than the typical $37,000 starting salary. But at the height of the high-tech boom, the Boston Public Schools were still having such a difficult time competing with private industry that district officials planned to negotiate salaries for new mathematics and science teachers that exceeded the top teacher pay allowable under the union contract.[11]

In Hartford, the teachers' union contract was also revised to permit the district to bring in new teachers in hard-to-staff subject areas at higher steps on the salary schedule.[12] But the change has led to unintended consequences that have angered many longtime district employees. Some of the newly hired teachers are being offered higher salaries than experienced veterans are currently earning, because incumbent teachers were forced to forego step increases during 3 salary freezes and they did not receive credit for student teaching or substitute teaching under the terms of the old contract. Some of the incumbents have pointed out that they could earn up to $10,000 more simply by quitting their jobs and reapplying for their positions. The Hartford Federation of Teachers estimates that this unusual pay disparity could affect 30 to 40 percent of the city's teachers, and it has filed a grievance which could take years to resolve. If the district is ordered to increase salaries for teachers hired under the old pay schedule, the district might have to cut programs, lay off teachers, or freeze the salaries of newly hired teachers until they are in line with the salaries of longtime staff. Former union president Edwin Vargas warned of an additional hidden cost if Hartford's veteran teachers opt to rectify the pay disparity by switching districts: "If Hartford loses teachers to the suburbs, they're going to lose experienced people, and they'll hire inexperienced people at a higher salary. . . . If they're going to be competitive with the new, they can't mistreat the old."[13]

BONUSES

Bonuses are a simpler way to compensate teachers at higher rates of pay because they do not require districts to renegotiate union contracts. One problem with bonuses, though, is that they are highly vulnerable to funding cuts when state economies are weak because the programs are added on top of the normal teacher salary schedule.[14] Bonuses to recruit and retain teachers generally fall into 4 categories: signing bonuses, bonuses for additional skills and knowledge, bonuses for critical subject area shortages, and bonuses for teachers willing to work in low-performing or hard-to-staff schools. Bonus pay for raising student achievement is another form of alternative compensation that is not addressed here because its usual purpose is to motivate teachers to change their performance, not to change the distribution of teachers across schools.

Signing bonuses. A number of districts offer up-front signing bonuses, as do 4 states: Maryland, Massachusetts, New York, and South Carolina.[15] Houston even pays teachers with at least 3 years of experience $3,000 retention bonuses to keep the teachers it already has.[16] In North Carolina, one district pays its employees unlimited $100 finder's fees for every certified teacher they recommend that is eventually hired.[17] In New Orleans, where more than 700 classroom teachers are uncertified, the school district is soliciting donations from local businesses so that the district can offer $1,000 to $5,000 signing bonuses to attract fully certified teachers.[18]

The bonus program that has attracted the most attention is the Massachusetts Signing Bonus Program for New Teachers. The program awards $20,000 bonuses to mid-career professionals who complete alternative certification through the Massachusetts Institute for New Teachers (MINT) program and teach full-time in public schools for 4 years. The program is the only one in the country to offer signing bonuses to individuals who have never before taught in public schools.[19]

Bonuses for additional skills and knowledge. At present, 33 states and 351 school districts offer salary supplements for accomplished teachers who achieve national certification from the National Board for Professional Teaching Standards.[20] Of these, only 1 district and 3 states offer additional monetary incentives to encourage National Board certified teachers to teach in low-performing schools.

National Board certified teachers in Fairfax County, Virginia, can increase their annual pay by $3,500 by taking on additional responsibilities and working in schools that serve large numbers of disadvantaged students.[21] National Board certified teachers in Florida are eligible for annual $1,000 bonuses each year they teach in the state's lowest performing Grade F schools.[22] In addition to their regular salary, National Board certified teachers in New York receive annual stipends of $10,000 for up to 3 years if they teach in low-performing schools and mentor new teachers.[23] In California, every National Board certified teacher receives a one-time bonus of $10,000. However, those who agree to work in schools in the bottom half of the state's academic performance list receive an additional $20,000 ($5,000 a year for 4 years).[24] During the 2000–2001 school year (the first year of the bonus program), nearly half of California's National Board certified teachers (356 out of 781) taught in low-performing schools. State officials estimated that during the following year, about 60 percent of the candidates for National Board certification were teaching in low-performing schools.[25]

To increase the numbers of National Board certified teachers in high-poverty, low-performing schools, U.S. Representative Susan Davis (D-CA) introduced H.R. 4599 in April 2002, the *National Board-Certified Teachers in Low-Performing Schools Act.*[26] The proposed legislation would provide $20,000 stipends ($5,000 a year for up to 4 years) for as many as 100 National Board certified teachers willing to work in high-poverty, low-performing schools and help other teachers in those schools become National Board certified. The 100 teachers would receive an additional stipend of $1,000 for each teacher in their schools who completed the process for becoming National Board certified.

Some states and districts offer bonuses to accomplished teachers who achieve other forms of advanced certification. North Carolina gives 10 percent salary increases to teachers who earn advanced state certificates. Maryland teachers who hold an Advanced Professional Certificate and teach in low-performing schools designated as "challenge, reconstitution-eligible, or reconstituted schools" earn $2,000 bonuses.[27] More than 2,700 Maryland teachers are receiving these bonuses by agreeing to teach in the target schools for 3 years.[28]

In some cases, monetary rewards for additional skills and knowledge are extended to beginning teachers who graduate at the top of their classes. In Houston, new teachers with grade-point averages of 3.0 or higher receive $500 bonuses.[29] In Maryland, teachers who graduate in the top 10 percent of their classes and serve in public schools for at least 3 years receive bonuses of $1,000.[30]

Critical subject area shortages. New teachers with specializations in high-demand subject areas receive $5,000 bonuses in Houston.[31] The Los Angeles Unified School District offers $5,000 bonuses to bilingual teachers.[32] In New York, the state pays $3,400 bonuses to teachers in critical subject shortage areas for up to 4 years.[33] Mathematics and science teachers who agree to remain in Utah districts for at least 4 years receive one-time bonuses of $5,000.[34] Florida and Georgia have also enacted legislation to offer bonus pay to teachers in high-need subject areas, although neither state is reported to be offering the bonuses at this time.[35]

Low-performing/hard-to-staff schools. Philadelphia offers $2,000 to teachers willing to work in 19 hard-to-staff schools.[36] Experienced teachers in Louisiana who transfer to the state's 11 lowest-performing schools in New Orleans receive $2,500 bonuses in addition to 125 hours of professional development.[37] The Winston-Salem/Forsyth County school district in North Carolina offers bonuses equal to 20 percent of the local salary supplement to teachers who work in the district's neediest schools for a full year.[38] Florida awards annual bonuses of up to $3,500 to high-quality teachers who teach in the state's lowest-performing schools.[39] Middle and high school teachers certified in mathematics, science, and special education who agree to teach in high-poverty or low-performing schools earn $1,800 bonuses in North Carolina.[40]

Several states in the South have also implemented incentive programs that provide salary supplements to experienced teachers for assisting low-performing schools. In South Carolina, participants in the state's Teacher Specialist On-Site Program receive $19,000 in additional pay, an amount equivalent to half the average annual teacher salary in the South.[41] Kentucky's Highly Skilled Educators program and Louisiana's Distinguished Educator program pay participating teachers 135 percent of their regular salaries for assisting low-performing schools. Alabama pays Special Service teachers $5,000 bonuses through a similar program.[42]

HOUSING INCENTIVES

A wide variety of housing incentives have been created to help schools attract and retain teachers. Housing incentives started at the district level, but states, the federal government, and private industry are also experimenting with a variety of incentives to increase teacher compensation by making housing more affordable, particularly in areas with high housing costs. The broad range of housing incentives available includes relocation assistance, reduced or free rent and utilities, teacher housing, housing loans and grants, reduced-price homes, low-interest mortgages, assistance with down payments and closing costs, and tax credits. A number of these programs are targeted specifically to teachers and principals who agree to work in low-performing schools or in urban areas, where housing costs tend to be higher and schools tend to have greater difficulty filling teacher vacancies.

Housing incentives have a number of distinct advantages as recruitment and retention tools:

- They are popular among state policymakers, who view non-salary incentives such as housing assistance as an additional way to increase their state's competitiveness.[43]
- They are extra perks that recruiters can use to promote their school district and attract teachers that may actually cost the district nothing.

- They can help districts in areas with high housing costs overcome the difficulty of home ownership, which can be one of the biggest barriers to recruiting teachers.[44]
- They can help rural districts attract and retain teachers in remote areas.
- They connect teachers to the community and enable teachers to teach in schools close to their homes.
- And they can help decrease staff turnover, because teachers who buy homes in the community are less likely to leave the school district.

Relocation assistance. Covering the costs of moving expenses is one of the newest perks being offered to teacher recruits. Baltimore offers $1,000 loans to teachers who relocate from another state.[45] Teachers who buy homes in Baltimore are also eligible to receive $1,200 relocation grants to cover moving expenses, as well as $5,000 toward closing costs.[46]

The Critical Teacher Shortage Act of 1998 authorized Mississippi to provide relocation reimbursement grants of up to $1,000 in moving expenses to licensed teachers willing to move to areas of the state experiencing the most severe shortages of teachers.[47] The state department of education reports that 377 teachers have accepted the relocation grants thus far.[48]

Reduced or free rent and utilities. Reduced or free rent and utilities are other ways to help make teaching more affordable. Some districts have worked with apartment complexes to waive security deposits or utility hookup fees for teachers.[49] In Chicago, where residency rules formerly required all teachers to live in the city, the school board launched a three-month study to explore ways to keep the cost of living from becoming prohibitive, including reduced rent for classroom teachers and dormitories for those who were student teaching.[50] The New York City Board of Education pays the rent for aspiring teachers participating in a program that assigns them to student-teach primarily in poor, hard-to-staff districts such as East New York and Brownsville, Brooklyn.[51] In Baltimore, businesses and a foundation have joined forces to renovate an apartment building that will offer reduced rent for new teachers for up to 2 years.[52] And in rural Tintic, Utah, the school district has been paying the first year's rent and all utilities except telephone bills for any teacher willing to work in its most remote schools, a practice dating back 10 to 12 years. Retaining teachers in the district has been such a serious concern that Superintendent Patricia Rouse even persuaded the school board to buy a new four-bedroom house to rent to one popular teacher who was considering leaving because his family of seven had been living in a two-bedroom apartment.[53]

Florida is unique in that it has developed a statewide apartment discount program for public school teachers in partnership with one of the largest apartment owners in the state. Florida's "Equity for Education" program offers 10 percent discounts on monthly rent, reduces move-in fees by $100, waives application fees, and allows teachers to apply up to 20 percent of their monthly rent toward the purchase of a new home.[54]

Teacher housing. In a few cases, school districts are opting to build their own housing for teachers. The Bellevue, Washington, school district near Seattle hopes to become one of them. Because Washington has a statewide salary schedule, districts in areas with higher costs of living are losing teachers to communities with more affordable housing. Still, a recent proposal to provide housing allowances for teachers was turned down by state legislators. According to the district's superintendent, Mike Riley, "In Bellevue, the average house goes for $412,000, and we have the same salary schedule as the rural towns where you can buy a house for $150,000. . . . In addition to losing teachers to corporate America, which every district goes through, we're losing them to districts that are just enough away from the Seattle metropolitan area that they're into affordable homes."[55] To address this problem, Superintendent Riley has proposed using district-owned land (originally intended for additional schools that are no longer needed) to build affordable housing for teachers.

In Santa Fe, New Mexico, teacher housing is available courtesy of local high school students.[56] Although students in Santa Fe High School's building-trades program had been designing, building, and selling houses since the mid-1970s, the program became one-of-a-kind in 1998 when it shifted to building houses for district teachers. When one student-built home constructed on donated land did not sell during the school year, the district opted to buy the house and rent it to a teacher. The district purchased land for the building-trades program to build 12 more homes and then decided to buy all of them to address the short-age of affordable housing for its employees. Because Santa Fe had be-come a highly desirable area drawing a large artistic community, prop-erty values and rents had skyrocketed beyond the reach of the teachers who worked there. Some teachers commuted 60 miles or more from more affordable areas of the state. As Edward Lee Vargas, the superin-tendent of Santa Fe at the time, pointed out, "This puts us at a disad-vantage because as soon as an opening happens closer to a teacher's home, they leave us." Although all district employees were eligible for the student-built homes, teachers received highest priority in the lottery system used to select tenants. Rent was set at 25 percent of the teacher's annual income, and the money was used for a fund to build more teacher housing. Eventually, Superintendent Vargas hoped to supple-ment the student-built homes with a 50-unit complex of apartments and townhouses for teachers that would be built by independent contractors and architects.

Two years ago, the San Francisco Unified School District was also proceeding with plans to build a 43-unit apartment complex for teach-ers on land owned by the district.[57] The $15 million complex was ex-pected to be completed by fall 2002 and would rent apartments for as little as $700 a month, compared to more than $1,600 a month charged for a typical one-bedroom apartment in the city. The district eventually abandoned the project when it met strong opposition. Residents near the proposed site voiced concerns about parking and increased traffic, and some teachers argued that the proposal did not address the real problem: inadequate salaries that did not enable teachers to live in the city.[58]

But not all teachers in California are opposed to teacher housing. Forty miles to the south, the Santa Clara Unified School District com-pleted construction of the first district-built teacher housing in Califor-nia in April 2002.[59] In Santa Clara, the average cost of a new home is around $400,000, but beginning teacher salaries range from $44,000 to $46,000. The district invested $6 million to build a 40-unit apartment complex for teachers, nurses, and counselors who have worked for the school district three years or less. The district already owned the land, which had been previously used for a school that is now closed, and rents the apartments for about half the price of comparable apartments in the area. A lottery eventually had to be held to select residents from among nearly 100 interested teachers.[60] Other school districts in the surrounding area, such as San Jose, Palo Alto, East Palo Alto, and La Honda-Pescadero, are also considering teacher housing.[61]

Housing loans and reduced-price homes. While helping teachers find affordable apartments and houses to rent may help attract new teachers to the district, helping them buy a home increases the likelihood that they will stay. For this reason, the Santa Clara Unified School District also offers teachers low-cost housing loans through a corporate partnership with the computer-technology firm Intel, headquartered in Santa Clara. Intel agreed to the arrangement partly so that its own recruiters would be able to promote the high quality of the local school district as one of the benefits to its own employees.[62] Through this "equity share" agreement, teachers receive $500 a month loans toward their mortgage payments for 5 years, which they repay through the equity their homes accumulate. According to district officials, 12 teachers had settled on housing contracts and 3 more were pending at the end of the program's first year of operation.[63]

The Seattle School District and the neighboring Northshore School District have formed partnerships with a local bank, a Seattle nonprofit counseling agency, and Fannie Mae to create the Hometown Home Loan Program. The program offers low-interest home loans to teachers, as well as other related benefits, such as financial counseling and low down payments. Seattle Public School employees who purchase or refinance homes within the city limits also receive discounts on closing costs and become eligible for special programs. Seattle's program, created in 1996, has provided at least 121 home loans to school employees thus far. The new Northshore School District program began in March 2002, but by the end of the first month it had already approved 1 teacher for a home loan and had 2 more applications pending.[64]

In some urban districts, support from the city's department of housing has led to the creation of low-interest loans and other housing benefits for teachers. The city of San Jose, California, for example, created the Teacher Homebuyer Program in 2000. The program offers interest-free loans of up to $40,000 to help teachers in the city's public schools purchase homes. Since its inception, at least 140 public school teachers have received the loans.[65]

In 1997, Baltimore began offering $5,000 housing loans to all city employees, including teachers, through the Baltimore City Employee Home Ownership Program. Repayment was reduced by 10 percent each year that the homeowner remained a city employee, so that the loan was effectively converted to a grant at the end of 10 years. The program enabled over 260 city employees to purchase homes, and school district officials believed that the program helped Baltimore recruit teachers.[66] However, the program's website notes that the program was discontinued in December 2000 due to budgetary constraints.[67]

The California State Teachers' Retirement System (CalSTRS) and the California Housing Loan Insurance Fund (CaHLIF) recently teamed up to make home loans more accessible to teachers by creating a program called "80/17."[68] The program consists of an 80 percent first loan and a 17 percent "silent" second loan with deferred payments and simple interest, which means that teachers only have to qualify for a loan on 80 percent of the purchase price. The program was piloted in Los Angeles in May 2001 and was expanded statewide in November 2001. All employees in California public schools and members of the California State Teachers' Retirement System are eligible for the program.

Two states, California and Mississippi, have created home loan programs targeted specifically to teachers who work in hard-to-staff schools. In California, teachers and principals participating in the state's Extra Credit Teacher Home Purchase Program are guaranteed loans of $7,500 or more toward down payments, in addition to other program benefits such as reduced-rate mortgages. To qualify for the program, teachers and principals must agree to work at least 5 years in a low-performing school.[69]

Mississippi's Employer-Assisted Housing Teacher Program, created in 1998, provides forgivable housing loans to teachers who work in designated geographic areas experiencing severe shortages of teachers. Licensed teachers can receive loans of up to $6,000 toward the down payment and closing costs on a home. The loan is "forgiven" and converts to an interest-free grant if the teacher remains at least 3 years in a critical teacher-shortage district. The state department of education reports that at least 93 teachers have received the forgivable loans.[70]

The federal government sponsors a program that aims not only to reduce the cost of home ownership for teachers, but to attract teachers to live and work in urban communities. The Teacher Next Door program, administered by the U.S. Department of Housing and Urban Development, was created in 1999. It is based upon the Officer Next Door program, which was created 2 years earlier to draw police officers to economically distressed neighborhoods. The program sells federally owned homes in more than 600 designated revitalization areas at half price to any certified teacher or administrator employed full-time in a public school, private school, or educational agency. Teachers must work in the school district in which the home is located, and they must agree to live in the home for 3 years, but they do not have to be first-time homebuyers. More than 1,500 teachers have purchased homes through the Teacher Next Door program in 34 states and the District of Columbia.

Low-interest mortgages. Two states, Connecticut and California, offer low-interest mortgages as another strategy to recruit teachers to low-performing or hard-to-staff schools. Connecticut's Teachers Mortgage Assistance Program offers low-interest mortgages to certified teachers who teach in high-need school districts as well as those who teach high-demand subjects, such as mathematics, science, and special education. The program was created in 2000 "to address the state's teacher shortage and to help make urban school districts more competitive with suburban districts in terms of recruiting teachers," according to a spokesperson for the state department of education.[71] About a dozen Connecticut teachers received the mortgages during the first 6 months of the program.

California teachers are also eligible for low-interest mortgages through the state's Extra Credit Teacher Home Purchase Program if they are first-time homebuyers and are willing to serve in low-performing schools for 5 years. The program was created in September 2000 and is sponsored by the California Debt Limit Allocation Committee (CDLAC). The program provides below-market interest rate mortgages through mortgage revenue bonds, which result in substantial savings to teachers at no cost to the school district. (Jurisdictions participating in the Extra Credit Teacher Home Purchase Program can also use their funds to offer tax credits instead of reduced interest rates, an alternative that will be discussed in the section on tax incentives.) Reducing a $150,000 mortgage through this program, for example, would decrease the teacher's interest rate by about 1 percent, a savings of approximately $37,000 over the life of the loan.[72] The program is administered through the California Housing Finance Agency and is available to all areas in the state, but highest priority for funding is given to cities and counties in California that provide matching funds and have the highest need for assistance recruiting and retaining certified teachers and principals. Participating jurisdictions include Los Angeles County, Orange County, and San Bernardino County, as well as the cities of Los Angeles and Oakland.

Assistance with down payments. Two corporate programs, Teacher Zero Down and Teacher Flex, were created by Bank of America in May 2000 to help teachers overcome one of the biggest barriers to purchasing a home, the down payment. The Teacher Zero Down program allows teachers with good credit to qualify for mortgages with no down payment. The Teacher Flex Program provides flexible guidelines and a 3 percent down payment for teachers who do not have an established credit or job history because they have recently graduated and are just beginning their careers.

Public- and private-school teachers, administrators, librarians, and school-based health care specialists such as nurses, speech and language therapists, and counselors are eligible to participate. The mortgage programs are available in 36 states and the District of Columbia where Bank of America has banking centers or mortgage sales offices. During the first 8 months the programs were in operation, 1,117 educators participated: 379 teachers borrowed $52.5 million through the Teacher Flex program and 738 teachers borrowed $87.5 million through the Teacher Zero Down program between May and December 2000.[73]

In California, teachers can buy a house with a down payment of only $500 through the California Educator Program. The program is administered by Wells Fargo Bank, in partnership with the California Housing Loan Insurance Fund (CaHLIF), and Freddie Mac. Like the Teacher Flex program, the California Educator Program is particularly helpful to beginning teachers because it has no minimum tenure requirement.[74] The California State Teachers' Retirement System (CalSTRS) also offers a "95-5" program that requires no down payment and allows teachers to qualify for a loan on 95 percent of the purchase price of a home.[75]

In Maryland, the Home Incentives for Teachers (HIT) program offers no-fee and no-down payment programs to teachers and administrators, in addition to savings on title fees, discounts on moving expenses, and cash bonuses on the sale and purchase of a home. Funding for the initiative is made possible by funds set aside for low-interest mortgages through the Department of Housing and Community Development's bond-funded homeownership program, but the program is not authorized or administered by the Maryland State Department of Education or the State of Maryland.[76]

TUITION ASSISTANCE

College scholarships and loans to attract more teaching candidates and reduce the costs of becoming a teacher are the most common types of monetary incentive that states offer, according to surveys conducted by *Education Week*.[77] In 2000, 27 states provided an average of $5,000 toward college tuition and expenses in exchange for commitments to teach in the public schools after graduation. However, only 10 of the 27 required recipients to work in hard-to-staff schools (Alaska, Arkansas, California, Illinois, Massachusetts, Mississippi, North Carolina, South Carolina, Tennessee, and Texas.)

Scholarships. Mississippi's Critical Needs Teacher Scholarship Program provides full scholarships to candidates who pledge to teach in areas of the state experiencing severe teacher shortages. Recipients must teach 1 year in a geographical shortage area for each year of scholarship assistance.[78]

State lawmakers in Virginia revised and expanded the state's Teaching Scholarship Loan Program during the 2000 legislative session to increase the number of scholarships for teacher candidates and to encourage them to teach in subject areas and locations where they are most needed. Upon graduation, program participants must teach in a Virginia public school with a high concentration of low-income students, in a rural or urban district with a teacher shortage, or in a high-demand subject area discipline. In addition, they must begin teaching during the first academic year after completing their degrees, and they must teach continuously in Virginia for the same number of years that they received tuition assistance.[79]

In April 2002, the Illinois House passed a bill to create the Teach Illinois Scholarship Program, one of the newest college scholarships designed to direct teachers to districts experiencing the most severe shortages of teachers.[80] If approved by the Senate, the program will offer free tuition to undergraduates who commit to teach for at least 5 years in elementary or secondary schools in Illinois with identified staff shortages.

Some states have also created scholarship programs to help teachers who are already in the workforce complete advanced degrees if they work in low-performing schools or shortage areas. Both Arkansas and Mississippi created University Assisted Teacher Recruitment and Retention Grant Programs to encourage already-licensed teachers to relocate to areas experiencing teacher shortages.[81] Arkansas offers $2,000-a-year scholarships toward a master's degree in education if the recipient teaches concurrently in a geographic shortage area. In Mississippi, participating teachers receive scholarships toward a master's degree and become eligible for reimbursement of moving expenses if they agree to move to a critical teacher shortage area and teach there for 5 years.

Loans and forgivable loans. The federal government offers several types of loan forgiveness to teachers who serve in low-income or subject-matter shortage areas upon completion of their degrees.[82] Up to 100 percent of federal Perkins loans can be cancelled by teaching in a low-income school for 5 years.[83] Repayment of federal Stafford Loans may be reduced by up to $5,000 if teachers work full-time for 5 consecutive years in a low-income school.[84] Stafford Loan recipients may also be eligible to defer repayment of their loans for up to 3 years by teaching full-time in a federally-designated teacher shortage area.[85] In addition, recipients of federal Douglas Scholarships may be eligible to reduce their repayment obligations by teaching in a federally approved teacher shortage area. Recipients are normally required to teach 2 years for every year of assistance received, but they are only required to teach 1 year for each year of assistance received if they teach in a shortage area.[86]

Alabama provides scholarship loans to mathematics and science teacher candidates who commit to teach for at least 5 years in grades and geographic areas with shortages of teachers.[87] Several states also offer forgivable loans, which convert to scholarships once teachers fulfill obligations to teach for a specified period of time in low-performing schools, hard-to-staff areas of the state, or high-demand subjects. In

Mississippi, for example, 1 year of tuition assistance is forgiven for every two semesters of teaching in a geographic shortage area or a hard-to-fill subject area. South Carolina forgives state loans and federal Perkins loans if teachers remain for at least 5 years in "critical needs schools" which enroll large percentages of poor students. In North Carolina, student loans obtained through the Prospective Teacher Scholarship Loan Program are forgiven after recipients teach for 4 years in North Carolina public schools, but the loans are forgiven faster—in three years—if recipients teach in low-performing public schools.[88]

California's Assumption Program of Loans for Education (APLE) assumes up to $11,000 of teachers' student loan payments if they teach in California schools full-time for 4 years. The state assumes an additional $4,000 in student loans if the individual also teaches in a low-performing school, and $4,000 more on top of that if the teacher is certified in mathematics, science, or special education.[89] The number of participating teachers has increased from 400 in 1998; to 5,500 in 1999; and to 6,500 in 2000 and 2001.[90]

TAX INCENTIVES

Another type of financial incentive that has caught the interest of a growing number of states is tax incentives. In Maryland, State Superintendent of Schools Nancy Grasmick proposed a $500 state income tax credit for all classroom teachers in 1998 as part of an incentive plan to attract new teachers to Maryland and improve retention rates.[91] Although the $500 tax credit proposal was not adopted, the state legislature did pass a tuition tax credit to reduce teachers' out-of-pocket training costs and improve teacher quality. Maryland's tuition tax credit allows all classroom teachers to reduce their annual state income tax liability by $1,500 to offset graduate tuition expenses required to maintain their state certification.[92]

In Louisiana, a bill has been introduced to the state legislature that would exempt certified teachers from state income taxes if they earn less than $36,800, the average teacher salary in the southern states.[93] In Georgia, lawmakers are considering 3 bills that would reduce or waive teachers' state tax liability. HB 1153 proposes that all full- or part-time elementary or secondary school teachers in public or private schools shall not be subject to state income taxes.[94] HB 1311 was recently introduced in the Georgia General Assembly for the purpose of amending the state tax code "so as to provide that income received by educators who contract to work at low-performing schools in this state shall not be subject to state income tax . . ." The legislation defines "qualifying educator" as one "who has contractually agreed to work for a period of 3 years at a low-performing school in this state."[95] The third bill, HB 573, allows an annual state income tax credit up to $2,000 per year for students who qualify for a PROMISE teacher's scholarship but are accepted into a teacher education program outside of Georgia. The tax credit is good for a period of up to 10 years as long as the teacher teaches in a public school in Georgia.[96]

California offers 2 different kinds of tax credits to teachers. The first is a state income tax credit of $250 to $1,500 per year for any credentialed California teacher in active service who has at least 4 years' teaching experience. This tax credit is offered to all teachers as an incentive to retain experienced credentialed teachers in the workforce. Teachers with 4 to 5 years' experience can claim a $250 state tax credit each year, teachers with 6 to 10 years' experience can claim a $500 tax credit, teachers with 11 to 19 years' experience can claim a $1,000 credit, and those teaching 20 years or more can claim a $1,500 tax credit. Revenue loss to the state is estimated at $188 million for 2001–2002 and $202 million for 2002–2003.[97] According to California Governor Gray Davis, "more than 200,000 teachers have taken advantage of our teacher tax credit."[98]

California also offers a second tax credit for educators through the Extra Credit Teacher Home Purchase Program. This housing incentive works as a federal income tax credit targeted to teachers and principals who work in high-poverty, low-performing schools. As explained in the section on low-interest mortgages, the program allows cities and counties to use mortgage revenue bonds, or in this case tax credits, to support a program to recruit and retain teachers and principals. To qualify, educators must be first-time home buyers and agree to serve for a minimum of 5 years in a low-performing school. The program is also called a mortgage credit certificate program, or MCC.

Four counties and 2 cities in California are using their funds to offer MCCs: Sacramento County, San Francisco County, Santa Clara

County, Santa Cruz County, and the cities of San Francisco and Oakland. The MCC allows eligible teachers and principals to reduce their tax liability by taking 15 percent of their annual mortgage interest payments as a dollar-for-dollar federal income tax credit. In Santa Clara County and in San Francisco City and County, recipients may claim a tax credit of 20 percent, rather than 15 percent. If the teacher or principal does not pay enough tax during the year to use the full credit, the unused credit can be carried over for up to 3 years. The program results in substantial savings to teachers and principals at no cost to the school district. For example, a teacher who has a $150,000, 8 percent fixed interest rate mortgage and claims 15 percent of the mortgage interest payment as a dollar-for-dollar tax credit can save approximately $1,800 in taxes annually and approximately $37,000 over the life of the mortgage. The credit would be highest in the early years of the loan, when more interest and less principal are paid.[99]

Other types of federal tax benefits targeted to teachers are also gaining interest among policymakers. The Bush Administration supports tax benefits targeted specifically to teachers, as evidenced by the inclusion of a new teacher tax deduction in the President's FY2003 budget. The teacher tax deduction, which President Bush signed into law in March 2002 as part of the economic stimulus bill, allows teachers to deduct up to $250 for out-of-pocket expenditures related to classroom instruction.[100]

In January 2002, the American Association of School Administrators proposed a federal income tax credit for fully certified teachers and principals willing to work in high-poverty, low-performing public schools.[101] Under AASA's proposed plan, teachers and principals who serve in these schools would be able to reduce their federal income tax payments by up to $4,000 a year. This strategy could make an enormous difference in the ability of poorer schools to attract highly qualified teachers and principals to schools with the greatest needs.

A similar tax credit proposal was introduced by U.S. Representative Heather Wilson (R-NM) in March 2002. H.R. 3889, the *Teacher Tax Credit Act*, would provide tax credits for teachers and principals who work in Title I schools.[102] Under this proposal, teachers, assistant teachers, principals, and assistant principals who work in an elementary or secondary Title I school could claim a $2,000 federal income tax credit.

And in August 2002, Senator Jay Rockefeller (D-WV) introduced S. 2844, the *Incentives to Educate American Children (I Teach) Act*.[103] This proposal would allow teachers who work in rural or high-poverty schools to claim a $1,000 annual, refundable federal income tax credit. Teachers in any school who achieve National Board Certification could also claim a $1,000 tax credit. Teachers who are National Board certified and teach in rural or high-poverty schools would be eligible for both tax benefits.

In all likelihood, local, state, and federal incentives to attract and retain teachers will continue to grow in popularity as a promising remedy to the teacher shortage. Though most are fairly new, some have been in place long enough to provide some insights into how incentives should be structured to maximize their effectiveness. The following chapter presents 9 lessons learned from incentive programs that have already been implemented.

NOTES

1. Olson, L. "Sweetening the pot." In *Education Week*. (2000, January). "Quality Counts 2000: Who should teach?" www.edweek.com/sreports/qc00/templates/article.cfm?slug=recruit.htm.

2. New York State Education Department. "Teachers of Tomorrow program information." www.highered.nysed.gov/kiap/TRDU/tot/totinfo.htm.

3. Shields, P. M., et al. (2001). *The status of the teaching profession 2001*. Santa Cruz, CA: The Center for the Future of Teaching and Learning. www.cftl.org/documents/2001report/completereport.pdf; CalTeach. "Incentive programs for teachers." www.calteach.com/rewards/in3.cfm?t=2.

4. "Scandalous education inequity." *The (San Jose) Mercury News*, editorial, August 8, 2002. www.bayarea.com/mld/mercurynews/news/opinion/3822673.htm.

5. CalTeach. "Incentive programs for teachers in low-performing schools." www.calteach.com/rewards/in3.cfm?t=3; Governor's Teaching Fellowship Program. www.calteach.com/incentives/governor_tfp.pdf.

6. CalTeach. "Incentive programs for teachers in low-performing schools." www.calteach.com/rewards/in3.cfm?t=3.

7. Shields, P.M., et al. (2001). *The status of the teaching profession 2001*. Santa Cruz, CA: The Center for the Future of Teaching and Learning. www.cftl.org/documents/2001report/completereport.pdf.

8. The Center for the Future of Teaching and Learning. (2000). *Teaching and California's future: The status of the teaching profession, 2000. An update*

to the Teaching and California's Future Task Force, summary report. Santa Cruz, CA: Author. www.cftl.org/documents/2000summary_report.pdf.

9. Tapia, S. T. "Perks lure teachers with full credentials: Anaheim City offers extras, such as help with moving costs and student loans, to beef up its staff." *Orange County Register*, July 5, 2001; National Commission on Teaching & America's Future. (2001, November/December). "Doing it right: Anaheim City Schools have 100 percent fully certified teachers." *Focus on Teaching Quality*, *I*(4). www.nctaf.org/whatsnew/FocusOnTeachingQuality_Dec2001 .htm; Rossi, R., B. Beaupre, & K. Grossman. "Other states do it better." *Chicago Sun-Times*, September 9, 2001. www.suntimes.com/output/news/cst-nws-2main09.html.

10. American Federation of Teachers. "Professional compensation for teachers." Resolution passed by the AFT Executive Council on February 6, 2001. www.aft.org/edissues/teacherquality/profcomp4tchrs.htm.

11. Bradley, A. "High-tech field luring teachers from education." *Education Week*, January 19, 2000. www.edweek.com/ew/ewstory.cfm?slug=19gap.h19.

12. Gottlieb, R. "For city teachers, time doesn't pay: New salary rules favor newcomers, union says." *Hartford Courant*, May 28, 2001, p. A1; National School Boards Association. "In Hartford, new teachers paid more than veterans." *School Board News*, July 17, 2001. www.nsba.org/sbn/01-jul/071701-2.htm.

13. Gottlieb, R. "For city teachers, time doesn't pay: New salary rules favor newcomers, union says." *Hartford Courant*, May 28, 2001, p. A1.

14. Cornett, L. M., & G. F. Gaines (2002). *Quality teachers: Can incentive policies make a difference?*, p. 11. Atlanta: Southern Regional Education Board. www.srcb.org/main/highered/leadership/quality_teachers.asp.

15. Clewell, B. C., K. Darke, T. Davis-Googe, L. Forcier, & S. Manes (2000, September). *Literature review on teacher recruitment programs*, p. 25. Report prepared for the U.S. Department of Education, Planning and Evaluation Service. Washington, D.C.: The Urban Institute. www.ed.gov/offices/OUS/PES/lit_review.pdf.

16. Rossi, R., B. Beaupre, & K. Grossman. "Other states do it better." *Chicago Sun-Times*, September 9, 2001. www.suntimes.com/output/news/cst-nws-2main09.html.

17. Southeast Center for Teaching Quality. (2002, January). *Recruiting teachers for hard-to-staff schools: Solutions for the Southeast and the nation*, p. 11. Chapel Hill, NC: Author. www.teachingquality.org/resources/pdfs/hard_to_staff_schools_regional_brief.pdf.

18. Hoff, D. "New Orleans soliciting businesses for bonuses." *Education Week*, May 1, 2002. www.edweek.com/ew/newstory.cfm?slug=33recruit.h21.

19. Massachusetts Department of Education. "Deadline approaching for new teacher signing bonus program." Press release, January 23, 2002. www .doe.mass.edu/news/news.asp?id=487; The Massachusetts Institute for New Teachers (MINT)/The Massachusetts Signing Bonus Program for New Teachers. doe.mass.edu/mint/overview.html.

20. National Board for Professional Teaching Standards. "State and local action." www.nbpts.org.

21. Mathews, J. "Virginia to trim teacher bonuses." *Washington Post*, November 20, 2001, p. B07.

22. Southeast Center for Teaching Quality. (2002, January). *Recruiting teachers for hard-to-staff schools: Solutions for the Southeast and the nation.* Chapel Hill, NC: Author. www.teachingquality.org/resources/pdfs/hard_to_ staff_schools_regional_brief.pdf.

23. National Board for Professional Teaching Standards. "State and local action." www.nbpts.org.

24. Rossi, R., B. Beaupre, & K. Grossman. "Other states do it better." *Chicago Sun-Times*, September 9, 2001. www.suntimes.com/output/news/cst-nws-2main09.html.

25. Personal communication, Kay Garcia, Professional Development Office, California Department of Education, January 2002.

26. H. R. 4599, *National Board-Certified Teachers in Low-Performing Schools Act of 2002* (introduced in House). http://thomas.loc.gov/home/ thomas.html; Office of U.S. Representative Susan Davis (D-CA). "Susan Davis introduces bill on teacher quality." Press release, April 26, 2002. www .house.gov/susandavis/press/pr042602teacherquality.htm.

27. Maryland State Department of Education. "Teacher incentives update." www.msde.state.md.us/factsndata/IncentivesUpdateWeb.htm; Gaines, G. F. (2000). *Teacher salaries and state priorities for education quality—A vital link*, p. 17. Atlanta: Southern Regional Education Board. www.sreb.org/main/ benchmarks2000/teachersalaries.asp.

28. Cornett, L. M., & G. F. Gaines (2002). *Quality teachers: Can incentive policies make a difference?*, p. 9. Atlanta: Southern Regional Education Board. www.sreb.org/main/highered/leadership/quality_teachers.asp.

29. Rossi, R., B. Beaupre, & K. Grossman. "Other states do it better." *Chicago Sun-Times*, September 9, 2001. www.suntimes.com/output/news/cst-nws-2main09.html.

30. Maryland State Department of Education. "Fact sheet 48: Quality Teacher Incentive Act." www.msde.state.md.us/fact%20sheets/fact48.html.

31. Rossi, R., B. Beaupre, & K. Grossman. "Other states do it better." *Chicago Sun-Times*, September 9, 2001. www.suntimes.com/output/news/cst-nws-2main09.html.

32. Olson, L. "Sweetening the pot." In *Education Week*. (2000, January). "Quality Counts 2000: Who should teach?" www.edweek.com/sreports/qc00/templates/article.cfm?slug=recruit.htm.

33. New York State Education Department. "Teachers of Tomorrow program information." www.highered.nysed.gov/kiap/TRDU/tot/totinfo.htm.

34. Hassel, B. (2002, May). *Better pay for better teaching: Making teacher compensation pay off in the age of accountability*. Washington, D.C.: Progressive Policy Institute. www.ndol.org/documents/Hassel_May02.pdf.

35. Southeast Center for Teaching Quality. (2002, January). *Recruiting teachers for hard-to-staff schools: Solutions for the Southeast and the nation*. Chapel Hill, NC: Author. www.teachingquality.org/resources/pdfs/hard_to_staff_schools_regional_brief.pdf.

36. Useem, B. *In middle schools, teacher shortage reaches crisis levels*. www.philaedfund.org/notebook/Teacher%20Shortage.htm.

37. Southeast Center for Teaching Quality. (2002, January). *Recruiting teachers for hard-to-staff schools: Solutions for the Southeast and the nation*. Chapel Hill, NC: Author. www.teachingquality.org/resources/pdfs/hard_to_staff_schools_regional_brief.pdf.

38. Southeast Center for Teaching Quality. (2002, January). *Recruiting teachers for hard-to-staff schools: Solutions for the Southeast and the nation*, p. 11. Chapel Hill, NC: Author. www.teachingquality.org/resources/pdfs/hard_to_staff_schools_regional_brief.pdf.

39. Gaines, G. F. (2000). *Teacher salaries and state priorities for education quality—A vital link*, p. 17. Atlanta: Southern Regional Education Board. www.sreb.org/main/benchmarks2000/teachersalaries.asp.

40. Cornett, L. M., & G. F. Gaines (2002). *Quality teachers: Can incentive policies make a difference?*, p. 10. Atlanta: Southern Regional Education Board. www.sreb.org/main/highered/leadership/quality_teachers.asp.

41. South Carolina State Department of Education. "Teacher Specialist program." www.myscschools.com/offices/sq/tsos/.

42. Gaines, G. F. (2000). *Teacher salaries and state priorities for education quality—A vital link*, p. 17. Atlanta: Southern Regional Education Board. www.sreb.org/main/benchmarks2000/teachersalaries.asp.

43. Bank of America. "Bank of America introduces Teacher Flex home loans: New mortgage helps make homeownership affordable for California teachers." Press release, April 12, 2000. www.bankofamerica.com/newsroom/press/press.cfm?PressID=press.2000041202.htm&LOBID=4.

44. Bank of America. "Affordable mortgages for teachers announced by Freddie Mac, Bank of America, California Treasurers Office: $200 million initiative introduces Bank of America's 'Teacher Flex mortgage, Zero-Down mortgages from California State Teachers Retirement System." Press release, April

10, 2000. www.bankofamerica.com/newsroom/press/press.cfm?PressID= 20000410.03.htm&LOBID=4.

45. Chmelynski, C. "Housing incentives help districts attract teachers." *School Board News*, September 18, 2001. www.nsba.org/sbn/01-sep/091801-3.htm.

46. Hirsch, E. (2001, February). *Teacher recruitment: Staffing classrooms with quality teachers*, p. 11. Denver: State Higher Education Executive Officers. www.sheeo.org/quality/mobility/recruitment.pdf.

47. Southeast Center for Teaching Quality. (2002, January). *Recruiting teachers for hard-to-staff schools: Solutions for the Southeast and the nation.* Chapel Hill, NC: Author. www.teachingquality.org/resources/pdfs/hard_ to_staff_schools_regional_brief.pdf; Gaines, G. F. (2000). *Teacher salaries and state priorities for education quality—A vital link*, p. 10. Atlanta: Southern Regional Education Board. www.sreb.org/main/benchmarks2000/ teachersalaries.asp.

48. Chmelynski, C. "Housing incentives help districts attract teachers." *School Board News*, September 18, 2001. www.nsba.org/sbn/01-sep/091801-3.htm.

49. Galley, M. "For sale: Affordable housing for teachers." *Education Week*, March 7, 2001. www.edweek.com/ew/ewstory.cfm?slug=25housing.h20.

50. Chmelynski, C. "Housing incentives help districts attract teachers." *School Board News*, September 18, 2001. www.nsba.org/sbn/01-sep/091801-3.htm.

51. Holloway, L. "New York City campaigns to attract new teachers." *New York Times*, November 9, 1999.

52. Gaines, G. F. (2000). *Teacher salaries and state priorities for education quality—A vital link*, p. 11. Atlanta: Southern Regional Education Board. www.sreb.org/main/benchmarks2000/teachersalaries.asp.

53. Chmelynski, C. "Housing incentives help districts attract teachers." *School Board News*, September 18, 2001. www.nsba.org/sbn/01-sep/091801-3.htm.

54. Florida Department of Education. "Crist announces apartment rental program for teachers." Press release, May 21, 2001. www.firn.edu/doe/ bin00031/releases01/010521b.htm.

55. Chmelynski, C. "Housing incentives help districts attract teachers." *School Board News*, September 18, 2001. www.nsba.org/sbn/01-sep/091801-3.htm.

56. Abercrombie, K. "District looks to students for solution to housing crunch." *Education Week*, January 13, 1999. www.edweek.com/ew/vol-18/18build.h18.

57. Archer, J. "San Francisco schools to build housing for teachers." *Education Week*, June 7, 2000. www.edweek.com/ew/ewstory.cfm?slug=39sf.h19.

58. Galley, M. "For sale: Affordable housing for teachers." *Education Week*, March 7, 2001. www.edweek.com/ew/ewstory.cfm?slug=25housing.h20.

59. Folmar, K. "School district builds homes for teachers." *The (San Jose) Mercury News*, April 19, 2002. Hayasaki, E. "District offers teachers shelter from housing." *Los Angeles Times*, August 5, 2002. www.latimes.com/news/local/la-me-housing5aug05.story.

60. Galley, M. "For sale: Affordable housing for teachers." *Education Week*, March 7, 2001. www.edweek.com/ew/ewstory.cfm?slug=25housing.h20; Chmelynski, C. "Housing incentives help districts attract teachers." *School Board News*, September 18, 2001. www.nsba.org/sbn/01-sep/091801-3.htm.

61. Folmar, K. "School district builds homes for teachers." *The (San Jose) Mercury News*, April 19, 2002.

62. Galley, M. "For sale: Affordable housing for teachers." *Education Week*, March 7, 2001. www.edweek.com/ew/ewstory.cfm?slug=25housing.h20.

63. Chmelynski, C. "Housing incentives help districts attract teachers." *School Board News*, September 18, 2001. www.nsba.org/sbn/01-sep/091801-3.htm.

64. "School employees get help with home buying." *Seattle Times*, March 27, 2002. seattletimes.nwsource.com/text/134426729_northshore27e.html; www.continentalinc.com/loans/hometownLending/Affiliation.asp?affiliationID=8.

65. Chmelynski, C. "Housing incentives help districts attract teachers." *School Board News*, September 18, 2001. www.nsba.org/sbn/01-sep/091801-3.htm.

66. Galley, M. "For sale: Affordable housing for teachers." *Education Week*, March 7, 2001. www.edweek.com/ew/ewstory.cfm?slug=25housing.h20; Live Baltimore Marketing Center. "Baltimore City Employee Homeownership Program (BCEHP)." www.encorebaltimore.org/homebuy/bcehp.html.

67. Live Baltimore Marketing Center. "Baltimore City Employee Homeownership Program (BCEHP)." www.encorebaltimore.org/homebuy/bcehp.html.

68. California Housing Finance Agency. "Home loans more accessible for school teachers." News release, November 28, 2001. www.chfa.ca.gov/info/press-releases/2001-1128.pdf.

69. Galley, M. "For sale: Affordable housing for teachers." *Education Week*, March 7, 2001. www.edweek.com/ew/ewstory.cfm?slug=25housing.h20.

70. Chmelynski, C. "Housing incentives help districts attract teachers." *School Board News*, September 18, 2001. www.nsba.org/sbn/01-sep/091801-3.htm.

71. Galley, M. "For sale: Affordable housing for teachers." *Education Week*, March 7, 2001. www.edweek.com/ew/ewstory.cfm?slug=25housing.h20.

72. California State Treasurer's Office. "Extra Credit Teacher Home Purchase Program." www.treasurer.ca.gov/csfa/extracredit/details.htm.

73. Bank of America. "More than 1,100 educators purchased new homes in Year 2000 thanks to Bank of America Teacher Flex and Teacher Zero Down mortgage programs." Press release, March 27, 2001. www.bankofamerica.com/newsroom/press/press.cfm?PressID=press.20010327.03.htm.

74. Wells Fargo. "Wells Fargo Home Mortgage, CaHLIF and Freddie Mac address lack of affordable housing for California's teachers; announce new loan program." Press release, August 14, 2000. www.wellsfargo.com.

75. California State Teachers' Retirement System (CalSTRS). "CalSTRS home loan program." www.calstrs.ca.gov/benefit/homeloan/homeloan.html; Los Angeles Unified School District. "Los Angeles Teachers Mortgage Assistance Program." www.lausd.k12.ca.us/orgs/latmap/.

76. Maryland State Department of Education. "Teacher incentives update: Homeownership opportunities for teachers." www.msde.state.md.us/factsndata/IncentivesUpdateWeb.htm.

77. "Incentives and recruitment: Policy tables." In *Education Week*. (2000, January). "Quality Counts 2000: Who should teach?" http://edweek.com/sreports/qc00/tables/incentives-t1.htm.

78. Southeast Center for Teaching Quality. (2002, January). *Recruiting teachers for hard-to-staff schools: Solutions for the Southeast and the nation*. Chapel Hill, NC: Author. www.teachingquality.org/resources/pdfs/hard_to_staff_schools_regional_brief.pdf.

79. Education Commission of the States. (2000, Spring-Summer). Teaching quality—Hard-to-staff schools: Virginia's Teaching Scholarship Loan Program. *State Education Leader*, (18)2. www.ecs.org/clearinghouse/11/87/1187.htm.

80. McDermott, K. "House passes bill to give future teachers free tuition." *St. Louis Post-Dispatch*, April 2, 2002; State of Illinois, 92nd General Assembly Legislation, House Bill 0582. www.legis.state.il.us/legislnet/legisnet92/hbgroups/hb/920HB0582LV.html.

81. Southeast Center for Teaching Quality. (2002, January). *Recruiting teachers for hard-to-staff schools: Solutions for the Southeast and the nation*. Chapel Hill, NC: Author. www.teachingquality.org/resources/pdfs/hard_to_staff_schools_regional_brief.pdf.

82. U.S. Department of Education. "Cancellation/deferment options for teachers." www.ed.gov/offices/OSFAP/Students/repayment/teachers/index.html.

83. U.S. Department of Education. "Perkins Loan cancellation." www.ed.gov/offices/OSFAP/Students/repayment/teachers/perkins.html.

84. U.S. Department of Education. "Stafford Loan cancellation for teachers." www.ed.gov/offices/OSFAP/Students/repayment/teachers/stafford.html.

85. U.S. Department of Education. "Deferments for FFEL and Direct Loans." www.ed.gov/offices/OSFAP/Students/repayment/teachers/dlffel.html.

86. U.S. Department of Education. "Teaching reduced service requirement for Douglas Scholars." www.ed.gov/offices/OSFAP/Students/repayment/teachers/douglas.htm.

87. Southeast Center for Teaching Quality. (2002, January). *Recruiting teachers for hard-to-staff schools: Solutions for the Southeast and the nation.* Chapel Hill, NC: Author. www.teachingquality.org/resources/pdfs/hard_to_staff_schools_regional_brief.pdf.

88. Southeast Center for Teaching Quality. (2002, January). *Recruiting teachers for hard-to-staff schools: Solutions for the Southeast and the nation,* p. 5. Chapel Hill, NC: Author. www.teachingquality.org/resources/pdfs/hard_to_staff_schools_regional_brief.pdf

89. CalTeach. "Incentive programs for teachers in low-performing schools." www.calteach.com/rewards/in3.cfm?t=3.

90. Shields, P. M., et al. (2001). *The status of the teaching profession 2001.* Santa Cruz, CA: The Center for the Future of Teaching and Learning. www.cftl.org/documents/2001report/completereport.pdf.

91. Maryland State Department of Education. "New incentives announced to attract and retain quality teachers." Press release, October 27, 1998. www.msde.state.md.us/pressreleases/1998/october/1998-1027b.html.

92. Maryland State Department of Education. "Teacher incentives update." www.msde.state.md.us/factsndata/IncentivesUpdateWeb.htm.

93. Kuriloff, A. "Proposal seeks relief for teachers: Many would be freed from income taxes." *The (New Orleans) Times-Picayune,* March 14, 2002. www.nola.com/education/t-p/index.ssf?/newsstory/r_johntax14.html.

94. Georgia General Assembly, House Bill 1153. www2.state.ga.us/Legis/2001_02/fulltext/hb1153.htm.

95. Georgia General Assembly, House Bill 1311. www2.state.ga.us/Legis/2001_02/fulltext/hb1311.htm.

96. Georgia General Assembly, House Bill 573. www2.state.ga.us/Legis/2001_02/fulltext/hb573.htm.

97. Governor's Office. (2000, July). *State budget: Budget highlights, 2000–01.* Sacramento, CA: Author. Cited in The Center for the Future of Teaching and Learning. (2000). *Teaching and California's future: The status of the teaching profession 2000. An update to the Teaching and California's Future Task Force.* Santa Cruz, CA: Author. www.cftl.org/documents/2000complete_report.pdf.

98. Governor's address, California Governor Gray Davis, January 08, 2002. www.nga.org/governors/1,1169,C_SPEECH^D_3012,00.html.

99. California State Treasurer's Office. "Extra Credit Teacher Home Purchase Program." www.treasurer.ca.gov/csfa/extracredit/details.htm.

100. Fogarty, T. "Economic stimulus bill gives teachers a tax break." *USA Today*, March 19, 2002. www.usatoday.com/money/perfi/taxes/2002/03-15-teacher-relief.htm.

101. American Association of School Administrators. "American Association of School Administrators' report shows link between quality of educators and student achievement." Press release, January 16, 2002. www.aasa.org/newsroom/2002/jan/01-16-02_strong_america.htm; American Association of School Administrators. "American Association of School Administrators calls on President Bush to use State of the Union to strengthen economy by strengthening schools." Press release, January 29, 2002. www.aasa.org/newsroom/2002/jan/01-29-02.htm.

102. H. R. 3889, *Teacher Tax Credit Act of 2002* (introduced in House). thomas.loc.gov/home/thomas.html; Office of U.S. Representative Heather Wilson (R-NM). "Wilson aims to give teachers credit." Press release, March 8, 2002. wilson.house.gov/NewsCenter.asp.

103. S. 2844, *Incentives to Educate American Children (I Teach) Act of 2002* (introduced in Senate). http://thomas.loc.gov/home/thomas.html; Office of U.S. Senator Jay Rockefeller (D-WV). "Making teachers a top priority, Rockefeller aims to support teacher certification and commitment to rural and low-income schools." Press release, August 1, 2002. http://rockefeller.senate.gov/2002/pr080102.html.

CONCLUSIONS
AND RECOMMENDATIONS

Offering financial incentives to teachers willing to take on more challenging assignments is essential if we are to staff every school with highly qualified teachers. Compelling evidence suggests that most teachers do not choose to work in the most difficult schools voluntarily and will not work in them involuntarily. Changing the way that teachers are paid is a critical part of an overall strategy to attract and retain teachers in the schools that serve students with the greatest needs. All indicators suggest that paying teachers more money to take on jobs that are substantially harder is a necessary part of the solution. In short, incentives matter.

As has been shown, states and districts are implementing a broad range of financial incentives to recruit and retain teachers. Many of these programs are fairly new, and limited information is available to judge their effectiveness. However, preliminary participation rates indicate that financial incentives are attracting teachers' attention and are drawing teachers to schools that they might not have considered otherwise. The 600 New York City teachers who applied for transfers to the city's 39 lowest-performing schools when they were offered 15 percent pay raises are but one example.

Clearly, educational and political leaders will need much better information to understand how effective the various incentives are at recruiting and retaining an amply supply of high-quality teachers and channeling them to the schools where they are needed most. But there are already several important lessons learned from the incentive programs that have been implemented.

LESSONS LEARNED

1. The incentive has to be large enough to matter.[1]

One of the criticisms aimed at many of the earlier incentive programs is that they were generally too modest in scope to be motivating.[2] How big the incentives will have to be in order to be effective is obviously an important empirical question for policymakers and school system leaders. As a general rule, policymakers should aim to affect behavior on the margin. This means that financial incentives do not have to be so large that they will attract every teacher to high-poverty, low-performing schools. But the incentives should be large enough to capture the attention of those teachers who could be swayed, with appropriate rewards and support, to accept the challenge of working in the target schools.

Preliminary evidence suggests that if *purely* monetary incentives were offered, the increase in pay would have to be sizeable to attract enough certified teachers. In New York City, for example, the nonprofit Citizens Budget Commission recommended that the city increase teacher salaries by up to 25 percent in the lowest-performing schools, because the 15 percent pay increase offered in 39 of the SURR schools did not seem to be drawing sufficient numbers of certified teachers.[3] Hanushek et al. (2001) conclude that pay raises of 20, 30, or even 50 percent may be needed to offset the disadvantages that some schools face in the teacher labor market.[4] However, the size of the salary increase need not be as large if steps are taken to improve working conditions or increase the relative attractiveness of these schools in other ways, because compensation is only one of many job attributes that matter to teachers.

2. The incentive must be targeted to encourage educators to work in the schools where they are needed most.

As a general rule, teachers are not likely to seek out teaching positions in hard-to-staff schools unless the incentive requires it. The Massachusetts

Signing Bonus Program, for example, has been criticized because fewer than half of the first year's participants ended up teaching in urban schools, where the need to fill vacancies is greatest. However, teaching in urban schools was never a program requirement—it was merely encouraged.[5]

3. The incentive should impose a repayment penalty for failing to uphold the terms of the agreement.

The Massachusetts Signing Bonus Program has been further criticized for its high rate of teacher turnover, with an attrition rate the first year that was slightly higher than double the national average. But the incentive is structured so that participants receive $8,000 during the first semester of teaching and $4,000 in each of the following three years, with no obligation to repay the funds if they drop out.[6] Given the structure of this incentive, it should not be particularly surprising that 4 of the 63 initial participants dropped out before entering a classroom, 12 left after the first year, and 1 dropped out the following year.[7]

4. The incentive should spread out the bonus payments over several years, with the biggest payoff coming in later years.

Harvard professor of education Richard Murnane believes that Massachusetts could have structured its bonus program far more effectively by paying out $15,000 of the $20,000 bonuses in the third through fifth years after program participants had been in the classroom long enough to become experienced teachers, and only to those who had proven their effectiveness by passing rigorous performance evaluations. The remaining $5,000 could have been used for professional development and mentoring.[8]

Anthony Bryk, director of the Chicago Consortium on School Research, favors a similar approach with respect to bonuses.[9] He notes that one of the potential unintended consequences of up-front signing bonuses is that they may encourage teachers to hop from school to school to collect them, further aggravating the problem of high teacher turnover in low-achieving and hard-to-staff schools. Bryk recommends spreading the payments out, with the biggest payoff coming after teachers have been in the classroom for several years.

Financial incentives other than signing bonuses can also be spread out in this way to encourage retention. The Houston Independent School District, for example, awards veteran teachers up to $2,250 in additional pay for mentoring new teachers—but only if the teacher pairs remain in the same school for three years.[10] The veteran teacher earns $1,000 the first year, $750 the second year, and $500 the third year—a retention strategy that would probably be even more powerful if the bonus increased, rather than decreased, over time.

5. The incentive should be structured so that teachers are not penalized when school performance improves.

When financial incentives work as intended, they attract high-quality teachers to low-performing schools and keep them there long enough to raise overall school performance. However, incentives will work at cross-purposes if one of the conditions of receiving them is that the school continues to be low-performing. California has designed one solution to this problem. National Board certified teachers who agree to teach in low-performing California schools earn $5,000 bonuses per year, up to four years. If National Board certified teachers are assigned to a school that improves so that it is no longer designated as low-performing, the teachers still receive the bonuses for the entire four-year period. National Board certified teachers will also continue to qualify for the entire $20,000 bonus if they transfer to any other low-performing California public school. If they transfer to a school that is not low-performing during the four-year period, however, they will forfeit the remaining $5,000 bonuses.[11]

6. The incentive should be renewable.

Financial incentives should be viewed as a long-term strategy to attract high-quality teachers who can improve the performance of struggling schools over time. If high-quality teachers leave as soon as the incentive ends, chances are good that school performance will regress. It is important to note that the type of incentive offered at renewal does not have to be the same as the original. Offering to repay student loans, for example, may have strong appeal to beginning teachers, but once their loans are repaid this incentive will undoubtedly cease to motivate them. As the overall performance of the school improves, teachers may even prefer non-monetary incentives that offer new professional development and leadership opportunities, or incentives that recognize and reward their efforts in other ways.

7. More incentives should be designed to attract experienced teachers, rather than new recruits, to high-poverty, low-performing schools.

One of the chief reasons beginning teachers give for leaving the profession is placement in difficult assignments without adequate support.[12] Yet a number of current scholarship and loan programs, such as Virginia's Teaching Scholarship Loans, require recipients to begin teaching in high-poverty and hard-to-staff urban and rural schools during the first academic year after completing their degrees.[13] Unless there are sufficient numbers of experienced teachers who can support and mentor the new teachers in these schools, the incentive is not likely to hold these teachers. JoAnn Norris, head of the North Carolina Teaching Fellows program, concurs, noting:

> If you put a beginning teacher in a low-performing school building that you already know does not have the capacity to support beginning teachers, you have done a disservice. One of the things we're learning from our results on low-performing school buildings is that those schools already have a high proportion of beginning teachers. So I would suggest that is not good public policy.[14]

8. Incentive programs require state and/or federal support to sustain them and to maximize their effectiveness.

Although many districts are developing their own financial incentives to recruit new teachers, state and federal efforts are also needed to ensure that incentives offered by more affluent districts do not further stratify rich and poor. Only states can reallocate resources among districts to give poorer schools a fair chance to compete for good teachers. And some types of incentives, such as tax credits, must be initiated at the state and federal levels. Equity and governance issues aside, Shields et al. (1999) make the important point that districts simply do not have the capacity to make changes of the magnitude that will be required to solve the nation's teaching shortage:

> The production of teacher candidates must be coupled with efforts to improve the jobs they are expected to take and the compensation they are offered. Although districts . . . can work toward this goal to some degree, as well as do their part to tighten recruitment and hiring efforts, they cannot bear the burden of fixing the state's teacher crisis. Districts' actions may in

many cases aggravate the problem of too many underqualified teachers, but the problem is bigger and beyond the district unit. Districts—be they small or large, urban or rural—do not have the financial or human resources to fix working conditions enough or increase salaries enough to reach deeper into the larger supply of credentialed teachers. At best, they may siphon a few teachers away from another district.[15]

9. Incentive programs will require substantial reallocation of current resources as well as new money to be effective.

There is no doubt that ensuring quality education for poor and minority students will cost a substantial amount of money. Either we remove poor and minority students from poorly staffed schools and place them in schools with quality teachers elsewhere, or we place quality teachers in the students' neighborhood schools.

Failure to staff high-poverty, low-achieving schools with highly qualified teachers is apt to cost even more. If states fail to ensure that all schools meet the teacher quality provisions of *No Child Left Behind*, the federal government could withhold states' federal education funds.

In addition, local school districts are now required to pay the costs of private tutoring and transportation if parents request that their children be transferred out of failing schools. In 2002, over 8,600 public schools nationwide were considered failing under new federal guidelines.[16] In Chicago alone, busing students out of failing schools will cost $5 million in 2002–2003, and this cost will only cover students in 50 of the 179 eligible elementary schools who are being allowed to transfer to better schools.[17] If Chicago were to bus all students eligible for transfers, the cost would exceed $40 million.[18]

The increasing possibility of legal action is another consideration. More than 40 states have been sued for neglecting to provide adequate funding to poor school districts so that they could educate students to the standards specified in their own state laws. During the past 10 years approximately 20 states have been ordered by the courts to take steps to ensure that poor students have equal access to quality schools.[19]

In addition, the cost of continually recruiting and hiring teachers to replace those who leave is by no means cheap. Consider what public schools are already spending on administrative costs, marketing, public relations, and recruiting campaigns to replenish their supplies of teachers:

- A study by the Texas Center for Education Research estimates that high teacher turnover costs Texas school districts $329 million per year in administrative costs alone.[20]
- The Houston Independent School District spent $100,000 on radio, television, billboards, and newspaper advertising to attract new teachers during 2000–2001.[21]
- The Jefferson County Public Schools in Louisville, Kentucky, spent $120,000 on classified ads to recruit fully credentialed teachers in 2000–2001—twelve times the amount it had spent just five years earlier.[22]
- The Chicago Public Schools spent $5.1 million to recruit and hire 2,236 new teachers in 1999–2000, or $2,280 per new teacher. The district expected to spend an additional $5.7 million the following year to hire 3,000 more new teachers.[23]
- The New York City Board of Education began an $8 million advertising campaign in 2001 to recruit 10,000 new teachers, a cost of $800 per teacher in advertising alone.[24]
- At least 14 of the nation's largest urban school districts, including Chicago, Los Angeles, and New York City, are spending funds to recruit teachers overseas, particularly in critical-shortage subject areas such as mathematics, science, and world languages.[25]

These examples, of course, do not include the additional costs to students in terms of lost educational opportunities. For tens of thousands of students in poorly staffed schools, a highly qualified teacher can be a life-altering investment. When weighed against the costs of federal sanctions, lawsuits, and the hefty price of teacher attrition, financial incentives that have the potential to attract and retain teachers in the nation's most challenging classrooms should be considered an option well worth pursuing.

NOTES

1. Consortium for Policy Research in Education. "Emerging findings in teacher compensation." www.wcer.wisc.edu/cpre/tcomp/research/general/findings.asp .

2. Olson, L. "Sweetening the pot." In *Education Week*. (2000, January). "Quality Counts 2000: Who should teach?" www.edweek.com/sreports/qc00/templates/article.cfm?slug=recruit.htm.

3. Goodnough, A., & T. Kelley. "Newly certified teachers, looking for a job, find a paradox." *New York Times*, September 1, 2000.

4. Hanushek, E. A., J. F. Kain, & S. G. Rivkin (2001, November). *Why public schools lose teachers*, p. 19. Working Paper 8599. Cambridge, MA: National Bureau of Economic Research. www.nber.org/papers/w8599.

5. Massachusetts Department of Education. "The Massachusetts Institute for New Teachers (MINT): Overview." www.doe.mass.edu/mint/overview.html; Viadero, D. "Researcher: Teacher signing bonuses miss mark in Mass." *Education Week*, February 21, 2001. www.edweek.com/ew/ewstory.cfm?slug= 23bonus.h20.

6. Archer, J. "Mass. 'bonus babies' get crash course." *Education Week*, September 6, 2000. www.edweek.com/ew/ewstory.cfm?slug=01mabonus.h20.

7. Viadero, D. "Researcher: Teacher signing bonuses miss mark in Mass." *Education Week*, February 21, 2001. www.edweek.com/ew/ewstory.cfm?slug= 23bonus.h20.

8. Olson, L. "Sweetening the pot." In *Education Week*. (2000, January). "Quality Counts 2000: Who should teach?" www.edweek.org/sreports/qc00/ templates/article.cfm?slug=recruit.htm .

9. Rossi, R., B. Beaupre, & K. Grossman. "Other states do it better." *Chicago Sun-Times*, September 9, 2001. www.suntimes.com/output/news/cst-nws-2main09.html.

10. Markley, M. "Districts taking new steps to stem teacher turnover." *Houston Chronicle*, August 15, 2001.

11. California Department of Education. "National Board for Professional Teaching Standards in California." http://goldmine.cde.ca.gov/pd/nbpts/index .html.

12. Bolich, A. M. (2000). *Reduce your losses: Help new teachers become veteran teachers*. Atlanta: Southern Regional Education Board. www.sreb.org/ main/highered/reducelosses.asp.

13. Education Commission of the States. (2000, Spring-Summer). "Teaching quality—Hard-to-staff schools: Virginia's Teaching Scholarship Loan Program." *State Education Leader, 18*(2). www.ecs.org/clearinghouse/11/87/1187 .htm.

14. Olson, L. "Sweetening the pot." In *Education Week*. (2000, January). "Quality Counts 2000: Who should teach?" www.edweek.com/sreports/qc00/ templates/article.cfm?slug=recruit.htm.

15. Shields, P. M., et al. (1999). *The status of the teaching profession: Research findings and policy recommendations. A report to the Teaching and California's Future Task Force*. Santa Cruz, CA: The Center for the Future of Teaching and Learning. www.cftl.org/publications.html.

16. Henry, T. "Children will be able to transfer at 8,652 schools." *USA Today*, July 1, 2002. www.usatoday.com/news/education/2002-07-02-transfer .htm.

17. Grossman, K. "50 schools can send students to better ones." *Chicago Sun-Times*, July 30, 2002. www.suntimes.com/output/news/cst-nws-educ30.html.

18. Banchero, S., D. Rado, & A. B. Cholo. "Options to failing schools limited." *Chicago Tribune*, July 17, 2002.

19. "A visionary school plan in Maryland." *New York Times* editorial, April 30, 2002. www.nytimes.com/2002/04/30/opinion/_30TUE3.html?ex= 1021187043&ei=1&en=f5ee07341313321c.

20. Markley, M. "Districts taking new steps to stem teacher turnover." *Houston Chronicle*, August 15, 2001.

21. Hoff, D. "Urban districts employing more aggressive hiring tactics." *Education Week*, October 3, 2001. www.edweek.com/ew/newstory.cfm?slug= 05recruit.h21.

22. Hoff, D. "Urban districts employing more aggressive hiring tactics." *Education Week*, October 3, 2001. www.edweek.com/ew/newstory.cfm?slug= 05recruit.h21.

23. Johnston, R. "Chicago's efforts to recruit teachers pay off." *Education Week*, November 1, 2000. www.cdweck.com/ew/ewstory.cfm?slug=09chicago .h20.

24. Rossi, R., B. Beaupre, & K. Grossman. "Other states do it better." *Chicago Sun-Times*, September 9, 2001. www.suntimes.com/output/news/cst-nws-2main09.html.

25. Bradley, A. "Chicago makes deal with Feds to hire foreign teachers." *Education Week*, January 19, 2000. www.edweek.com/ew/ewstory.cfm?slug= 19gapside.h19; Archer, J. "Recruitment pinch fuels global trade in K–12 teachers." *Education Week*, February 14, 2001. www.edweek.com/ew/ ewstory.cfm?slug=22overseas.h20; Urban Teacher Collaborative. (2000). *The urban teacher challenge: Teacher demand and supply in the Great City Schools.* Belmont, MA: Author. www.rnt.org/quick/utc.pdf; Henry, T. "Teacher shortage gets foreign aid." *USA Today*, July 16, 2001. www.usatoday.com/news/nation/2001/07/16/teacher-shortage.htm; National School Boards Association. "School districts cast global net to fill teacher positions." *School Board News*, January 11, 2000. www.nsba.org/sbn/00-jan/011100-3.htm; Coeyman, M. "Come to America to teach. Sounds simple, right?" *The Christian Science Monitor*, June 25, 2002. www.csmonitor.com/2002/0625/ p15s01-lecl.htm.

RESOURCES ON THE WEB

BONUSES

State

California
Incentive programs for teachers
www.calteach.com/rewards/in3.cfm?t=2

National Board for Professional Teaching Standards Certification
Incentive Program
www.calteach.com/incentives/board_certified.pdf

Florida
Florida State Legislature, House Bill 0063
www.leg.state.fl.us/data/session/2000/House/bills/billtext/
pdf/h0063.pdf

Maryland
Reconstitution/Reconstitution-Eligible/Challenge School Stipend
www.msde.state.md.us/factsndata/IncentivesUpdateWeb
.htm

Signing Bonus
www.msde.state.md.us/factsndata/IncentivesUpdateWeb
.htm

Massachusetts
Massachusetts Signing Bonus Program for New Teachers,
Massachusetts Institute for New Teachers (MINT)
http://doe.mass.edu/mint/overview.html

New York
Teachers of Tomorrow, Recruitment Incentive Program
www.highered.nysed.gov/kiap/TRDU/tot/totinfo.htm

Teachers of Tomorrow, New York State Master Teacher Program
www.highered.nysed.gov/kiap/TRDU/tot/totinfo.htm

South Carolina
Teacher Specialist On-Site Program
www.myscschools.com/offices/sq/tsos/

Federal

H. R. 4599, *National Board-Certified Teachers in Low-Performing
Schools Act of 2002* (introduced in House)
http://thomas.loc.gov/home/thomas.html

Office of U.S. Representative Susan Davis (D-CA). "Susan Davis
introduces bill on teacher quality." Press release, April 26,
2002.
www.house.gov/susandavis/press/pr042602teacherquality
.html

HOUSING SUBSIDIES

City/County

Baltimore
Baltimore City Employee Homeownership Program (BCEHP)
www.encorebaltimore.org/homebuy/bcehp.html

Los Angeles
Los Angeles Teachers Mortgage Assistance Program
www.lausd.k12.ca.us/orgs/latmap/

San Jose
Teacher Home Buyer Program
www.sjhousing.org/program/thp.html

Santa Clara County
Santa Clara County Housing Bond Trust Fund Loan
www.mccprogram.com/hbtfa.html

Seattle
(Seattle School District and Northshore School District)
Hometown Home Loan Program
http://seattletimes.nwsource.com/text/134426729_northshore27e
   .html
www.continentalinc.com/loans/hometownLending/
   Affiliation.asp?affiliationID=8

State

California
www.homesforteachers.com

California State Teachers' Retirement System's Home Loan
   Program
www.calstrs.ca.gov/benefit/homeloan/homeloan.html

Extra Credit Teacher Home Purchase Program
www.treasurer.ca.gov/csfa/extracredit/details.htm

A. Reduced interest rate loan program
   • Statewide
      www.chfa.ca.gov/homeownership/programs/
         extracredit.htm
   • Los Angeles
      www.cityofla.org/LAHD/xtracred.htm
   • Los Angeles County
      www.lacdc.org/schfa/teachers/index.shtm

- Oakland
  www.chfa.ca.gov/homeownership/programs/
  oaklandteacher.htm
- Orange County
  www.lacdc.org/schfa/teachers/index.shtm
- San Bernardino County
  www.wolfhousing.com/programs.htm

B. Federal income tax credit (mortgage credit certificate) program
- Oakland
  www.co.alameda.ca.us/cda/mcc_program/what.htm
- Sacramento
  www.shra.org/housing/buyer/
  Teacher%20Home%20Purchase1.html
- San Francisco—City and County
  www.ci.sf.ca.us/moh/ecthpp/flyer.htm
- Santa Clara County
  www.mccprogram.com/teachermcc.html
- Santa Cruz County
  www.hacosantacruz.org/homebuyers/teachmcc.htm

Connecticut
Teachers Mortgage Assistance Program
www.chfa.org/FirstHome/firsthome_TeacherMortProgram.asp

Maryland
Home Incentives for Teachers (HIT)
www.msde.state.md.us/factsndata/IncentivesUpdateWeb.htm

Mississippi
Employer-Assisted Housing Teacher Program
www.mshc.com/single%20family/HAT/hat%20main.html
www.mshc.com/single%20family/HAT/HATsynop.pdf

Federal

U.S. Department of Housing and Urban Development (HUD):
Teacher Next Door program
www.hud.gov/offices/hsg/sfh/reo/tnd/tnd.cfm

Corporate

Bank of America: Teacher Zero Down and Teacher Flex
www.bankofamerica.com/loansandhomes/index.cfm?
template=lc_mort_special_teachers?statecheck=MD&detail=
TEACHERS&nav4=

Wells Fargo: California Educator Program
www.wellsfargo.com

TUITION ASSISTANCE

State

California

Governor's Teaching Fellowship Program (discontinued)
www.calteach.com/incentives/governor_tfp.pdf

Assumption Program of Loans for Education (APLE)
www.calteach.com/incentives/assumption.pdf

Illinois

Teach Illinois Scholarship Program (proposed)
www.legis.state.il.us/legislnet/legisnet92/hbgroups/hb/
920HB0582LV.html

Mississippi

Critical Needs Teacher Scholarship Program
www.mde.k12.ms.us/mtc/teach.htm

Mississippi Teacher Fellowship Program
www.mde.k12.ms.us/mtc/teach.htm

New York

Certification Stipends
www.highered.nysed.gov/kiap/TRDU/tot/totinfo.htm

Teacher Recruitment Tuition Reimbursement Program
www.highered.nysed.gov/kiap/TRDU/tot/totinfo.htm

North Carolina

Prospective Teacher Scholarship Loan
www.ncpublicschools.org/scholarships/ptsl.htm

Virginia
Teaching Scholarship Loan Program
www.pen.k12.va.us/VDOE/newvdoe/vtslp.htm

Federal

Cancellation/Deferment Options for Teachers
www.ed.gov/offices/OSFAP/Students/repayment/teachers/
index.html
- Douglas Scholarship reduced service obligations
  www.ed.gov/offices/OSFAP/Students/repayment/
  teachers/douglas.html
- Perkins Loan Cancellation
  www.ed.gov/offices/OSFAP/Students/repayment/
  teachers/perkins.html
- Stafford Loan Cancellation
  www.ed.gov/offices/OSFAP/Students/repayment/
  teachers/stafford.html
- Stafford Loan Deferment
  www.ed.gov/offices/OSFAP/Students/repayment/
  teachers/dlffel.html

TAX INCENTIVES

State

California
A. State income tax credit (Teacher Retention Credit)
   www.ftb.ca.gov/forms/misc/801.pdf
   California Tax Form 3505, Teacher Retention Credit
   www.ftb.ca.gov/forms/01_forms/01_3505.pdf

B. Federal income tax credit (mortgage credit certificate)
   available through the Extra Credit Teacher Home Purchase
   Program
   www.treasurer.ca.gov/csfa/extracredit/details.htm
   - Oakland
     www.co.alameda.ca.us/cda/mcc_program/what.htm

- Sacramento
  www.shra.org/housing/buyer/
     Teacher%20Home%20Purchase1.html
- San Francisco—City and County
  www.ci.sf.ca.us/moh/ecthpp/flyer.htm
- Santa Clara County
  www.mccprogram.com/teachermcc.html
- Santa Cruz County
  www.hacosantacruz.org/homebuyers/teachmcc.htm

Georgia

Georgia General Assembly, House Bill 573 (proposed)
www2.state.ga.us/Legis/2001_02/fulltext/hb573.htm

Georgia General Assembly, House Bill 1153 (proposed)
www2.state.ga.us/Legis/2001_02/fulltext/hb1153.htm

Georgia General Assembly, House Bill 1311 (proposed)
www2.state.ga.us/Legis/2001_02/fulltext/hb1311.htm

Louisiana

www.nola.com/education/t-p/index.ssf?/newsstory/r_johntax14.html

Maryland

Tuition Tax Credits
www.msde.state.md.us/factsndata/
   IncentivesUpdateWeb.htm

Federal

American Association of School Administrators
Leave No Child Behind Opportunity Tax Credit (proposed)
www.aasa.org/newsroom/2002/jan/01-16-02_strong_america
   .htm
www.aasa.org/newsroom/2002/jan/01-29-02.htm

H. R. 3889, *Teacher Tax Credit Act of 2002* (introduced in House)
http://thomas.loc.gov/home/thomas.html
   Office of U.S. Representative Heather Wilson (R-NM). "Wilson
   aims to give teachers credit." Press release, March 8, 2002.
   wilson.house.gov/NewsCenter.asp

S. 2844, *Incentives to Educate American Children (I Teach) Act of 2002* (introduced in Senate)
http://thomas.loc.gov/home/thomas.html
Office of U.S. Senator Jay Rockefeller (D-WV). "Making teachers a top priority, Rockefeller aims to support teacher certification and commitment to rural and low-income schools." Press release, August 1, 2002. http://rockefeller.senate.gov/2002/pr080102.html

REFERENCES

Abercrombie, K. "District looks to students for solution to housing crunch." *Education Week*, January 13, 1999. www.edweek.com/ew/vol-18/18build .h18.

American Association of School Administrators. "American Association of School Administrators calls on President Bush to use State of the Union to strengthen economy by strengthening schools." Press release, January 29, 2002. www.aasa.org/newsroom/2002/jan/01-29-02.htm.

American Association of School Administrators. "American Association of Administrators' report show link between quality of educators and student achievement." Press release, January 16, 2002. www.aasa.org/newsroom/ 2002/jan/01-16-02_strong.america.htm.

American Federation of Teachers. *AFT on the issues: Merit pay, "pay-for-performance," and professional teacher compensation.* www.aft.org/issues/ meritpay/meritpay.html.

American Federation of Teachers. "Professional compensation for teachers." Resolution passed by the AFT Executive Council on February 6, 2001. www.aft.org/edissues/teacherquality/profcomp4tchrs.htm.

Archer, J. "AFT to urge locals to consider new pay strategies." *Education Week*, February 21, 2001. www.edweek.com/ew/ewstory.cfm?slug=23aft.h20.

Archer, J. "Mass. 'bonus babies' get crash course." *Education Week*, September 6, 2000. www.edweek.com/ew/ewstory.cfm?slug=01mabonus.h20.

Archer, J. "Recruitment pinch fuels global trade in K–12 teachers." *Education Week*, February 14, 2001. www.edweek.com/ew/ewstory.cfm?slug=22overseas.h20.

Archer, J. "San Francisco schools to build housing for teachers." *Education Week*, June 7, 2000. www.edweek.com/ew/ewstory.cfm?slug=39sf.h19.

Associated Press. "Union sues over extra pay aimed at recruiting teachers." *St. Louis Post-Dispatch*, June 2, 2002.

Banchero, S., D. Rado, and A. B. Cholo. "Options to failing schools limited." *Chicago Tribune*, July 17, 2002.

Bank of America. "Affordable mortgages for teachers announced by Freddie Mac, Bank of America, California Treasurers Office: $200 million initiative introduces Bank of America's 'Teacher Flex' mortgage, Zero-Down mortgages from California State Teachers Retirement System." Press release, April 10, 2000. www.bankofamerica.com/newsroom/press/press.cfm?PressID=press.20000410.03.htm&LOBID=4.

Bank of America. "Bank of America introduces Teacher Flex home loans: New mortgage helps make homeownership affordable for California teachers." Press release, April 12, 2000. www.bankofamerica.com/newsroom/press/press.cfm?PressID=press.20000412.02.htm&LOBID=4.

Bank of America. "More than 1,100 educators purchased new homes in Year 2000 thanks to Bank of America Teacher Flex and Teacher Zero Down mortgage programs." Press release, March 27, 2001. www.bankofamerica.com/newsroom/press/press.cfm?PressID=press.20010327.03.htm.

Blair, J. "Districts wooing teachers with bonuses, incentives." *Education Week*, August 2, 2000. www.edweek.com/ew/ewstory.cfm?slug=43raid.h19.

Blair, J. "Lawmakers plunge into teacher pay." *Education Week*, February 21, 2001. www.edweek.com/ew/ewstory.cfm?slug=23salary.h20.

Bolich, A. M. (2000). *Reduce your losses: Help new teachers become veteran teachers*. Atlanta: Southern Regional Education Board. www.sreb.org/main/highered/reducelosses.asp.

Bradley, A. "Chicago makes deal with Feds to hire foreign teachers." *Education Week*, January 19, 2000. www.edweek.com/ew/ewstory.cfm?slug=19gapside.h19.

Bradley, A. "High-tech field luring teachers from education." *Education Week*, January 19, 2000. www.edweek.com/ew/ewstory.cfm?slug=19gap.h19.

Bruno, J. E. (2002, July 26). The geographical distribution of teacher absenteeism in large urban school district settings: Implications for school reform efforts aimed at promoting equity and excellence in education. *Education Policy Analysis Archives, 10* (32). http://epaa.asu.edu/epaa/v10n32/.

California Department of Education. "National Board for Professional Teaching Standards in California." http://goldmine.cde.ca.gov/pd/nbpts/index.html.

California Housing Finance Agency. "Home loans more accessible for school teachers." News release, November 28, 2001. www.chfa.ca.gov/info/press-releases/2001–1128.pdf.

California State Teachers' Retirement System (CalSTRS). "CalSTRS home loan program." www.calstrs.ca.gov/benefit/homeloan/homeloan.html.

California State Treasurer's Office. "Extra Credit Teacher Home Purchase Program." www.treasurer.ca.gov/csfa/extracredit/details.htm.

CalTeach. "Governor's Teaching Fellowship Program." www.calteach.com/incentives/governor_tfp.pdf.

CalTeach. "Incentive programs for teachers." www.calteach.com/rewards/in3.cfm?t=2.

CalTeach. "Incentive programs for teachers in low-performing schools." www.calteach.com/rewards/in3.cfm?t=3.

Carroll, S., R. Reichardt, and C. Guarino. (2000, October). *The distribution of teachers among California's school districts and schools*. MR-1298.0-JIF. Santa Monica, CA: RAND.

The Center for the Future of Teaching and Learning. (2000). *Teaching and California's future: The status of the teaching profession, 2000. An update to the Teaching and California's Future Task Force*. Santa Cruz, CA: Author. www.cftl.org/documents/2000complete_report.pdf.

The Center for the Future of Teaching and Learning. (2000). *Teaching and California's future: The status of the teaching profession 2000. An update to the Teaching and California's Future Task Force, summary report*. Santa Cruz, CA: Author. www.cftl.org/documents/2000summary_report.pdf.

Chmelynski, C. "Housing incentives help districts attract teachers." *School Board News*, September 18, 2001. www.nsba.org/sbn/01-sep/091801-3.htm.

Claycomb, C. (2000, Winter). High-quality urban school teachers: What they need to enter and to remain in hard-to-staff schools. *The State Education Standard*, pp. 17–20. www.nasbe.org/Educational_Issues/Articles/1_Winter2000/Claycomb%20article.pdf.

Clewell, B. C., K. Darke, T. Davis-Googe, L. Forcier, and S. Manes. (2000, September). *Literature review on teacher recruitment programs*. Report prepared for the U.S. Department of Education, Planning and Evaluation Service. Washington, D.C.: The Urban Institute. www.ed.gov/offices/OUS/PES/lit_review.pdf.

Coeyman, M. "Come to America to teach. Sounds simple, right?" *The Christian Science Monitor*, June 25, 2002. www.csmonitor.com/2002/0625/p15s01-lecl.htm.

Consortium for Policy Research in Education. "Emerging findings in teacher compensation." www.wcer.wisc.edu/cpre/tcomp/research/general/findings.asp.

Cornett, L. M., and G. F. Gaines. (2002). *Quality teachers: Can incentive policies make a difference?* Atlanta: Southern Regional Education Board. www.sreb.org/main/highered/leadership/quality_teachers.asp.

Darling-Hammond, L. (2000). *Solving the dilemmas of teacher supply, demand, and standards: How we can ensure a competent, caring, and qualified teacher for every child.* New York: National Commission on Teaching and America's Future. www.nctaf.org/publications/solving.pdf.

Dezmon, B. (Ed.). (2001, January). *Minority achievement in Maryland at the millennium.* Report prepared by the Achievement Initiative for Maryland's Minority Students (AIMMS) Steering Committee. Baltimore: Maryland State Department of Education. www.msde.state.md.us/minority/pdf_files/2002/min.pdf.

Education Commission of the States. (2000, Spring-Summer). Teaching quality—Hard-to-staff schools: Virginia's Teaching Scholarship Loan Program. *State Education Leader, 18*(2). www.ecs.org/clearinghouse/11/87/1187.htm.

Farkas, S., J. Johnson, and T. Foleno, with A. Duffett, and P. Foley. (2000). *A sense of calling: Who teaches and why.* New York: Public Agenda. Summary available online. www.publicagenda.org/specials/teachers/teachers.htm.

Florida Department of Education. "Crist announces apartment rental program for teachers." Press release, May 21, 2001. www.firn.edu/doe/bin00031/releases01/010521b.htm.

Fogarty, T. "Economic stimulus bill gives teachers a tax break." *USA Today*, March 19, 2002. www.usatoday.com/money/perfi/taxes/2002/03-15-teacher-relief.htm.

Folmar, K. "School district builds homes for teachers." *The (San Jose) Mercury News*, April 19, 2002.

Gaines, G. F. (2000). *Teacher salaries and state priorities for education quality—A vital link.* Atlanta: Southern Regional Education Board. www.sreb.org/main/benchmarks2000/teachersalaries.asp.

Galley, M. "For sale: Affordable housing for teachers." *Education Week*, March 7, 2001. www.edweek.com/ew/ewstory.cfm?slug=25housing.h20.

Georgia General Assembly, House Bill 573. www2.state.ga.us/Legis/2001_02/fulltext/hb573.htm.

Georgia General Assembly, House Bill 1153. www2.state.ga.us/Legis/2001_02/fulltext/hb1153.htm.

Georgia General Assembly, House Bill 1311. www2.state.ga.us/Legis/2001_02/fulltext/hb1311.htm.

Gittrich, G. "The certification disincentive: 'Reward' is often job at bad school." *New York Daily News*, April 24, 2001. www.nydailynews.com/2001/-04/-24/ News_and_Views/City_Beat/a-108495.asp.

Goodnough, A. "Levy offers higher salaries to staff the worst schools." *New York Times*, August 2, 2000. www.nytimes.com/library/national/regional/ 080200ny-levy-edu.html.

Goodnough, A. "Political memo: Levy is sparring with an old ally over direction of the City schools." *New York Times*, August 10, 2000.

Goodnough, A. "Strain of fourth-grade tests drives off veteran teachers." *New York Times*, June 14, 2001, p. A1.

Goodnough, A. "Union seeks more incentives to staff troubled schools." *New York Times*, August 12, 2000.

Goodnough, A., and T. Kelley. "Newly certified teachers, looking for a job, find a paradox." *New York Times*, September 1, 2000.

Gottlieb, R. "For city teachers, time doesn't pay: New salary rules favor newcomers, union says." *Hartford Courant*, May 28, 2001, p. A1.

Governor's address, California Governor Gray Davis, January 08, 2002. www..nga.org/governors/1,1169,C_SPEECH^D_3012,00.html.

Governor's Office. (2000, July). *State budget: Budget highlights, 2000–01.* Sacramento, CA: Author. *Cited in* Center for the Future of Teaching and Learning. (2000). *The status of the teaching profession 2000: An update to the Teaching and California's Future Task Force.* Santa Cruz, CA: Author. www.cftl.org/documents/2000complete_report.pdf.

Grace, M. "Teachers ducking certificates: Fear being assigned to bad schools." *New York Daily News*, April 24, 2001. www.nydailynews.com/2001/-04/-24/ News_and_Views/City_Beat/a-108498.asp.

Grossman, K. "50 schools can send students to better ones." *Chicago Sun-Times*, July 30, 2002. www.suntimes.com/output/news/cst-nws-educ30.html.

Grossman, K., B. Beaupre, and R. Rossi. "Poorest kids often wind up with the weakest teachers." *Chicago Sun-Times*, September 7, 2001. www.suntimes .com/output/news/cst-nws-main07.html.

Hanushek, E. A., J. F. Kain, and S. G. Rivkin. (2001, November). *Why public schools lose teachers.* Working paper 8599. Cambridge, MA: National Bureau of Economic Research. www.nber.org/papers/w8599.

Hassel, B. (2002, May). *Better pay for better teaching: Making teacher compensation pay off in the age of accountability.* Washington, D.C.: Progressive Policy Institute. www.ndol.org/documents/Hassel_May02.pdf.

Hayasaki, E. "District offers teachers shelter from housing." *Los Angeles Times*, August 5, 2002. www.latimes.com/news/local/la-me-housing5aug05 .story.

Haycock, K. (1998, Summer). Good teaching matters: How well-qualified teachers can close the gap. *Thinking K–16, 3*(2), 1–14. Washington, D.C.: The Education Trust.

Hayward, E. "Applications for teacher signing bonus drop." *Boston Herald*, January 30, 2002. www2.bostonherald.com/news/local_regional/mint01302002.htm.

Hayward, E. "Mass. teachers decry demise of mentor program, stipends." *Boston Herald*, June 14, 2002. www.bostonherald.com/news/local_regional/teac06142002.htm.

Helfand, D. "Garfield High teachers say they can deliver again." *Los Angeles Times*, July 18, 2001. www.latimes.com/news/local/la-000058754jul18.story.

Henry, T. "Children will be able to transfer at 8,652 schools." *USA Today*, July 1, 2002. www.usatoday.com/news/education/2002–07–02-transfer.htm.

Henry, T. "Teacher shortage gets foreign aid." *USA Today*, July 16, 2001. www.usatoday.com/news/nation/2001/07/16/teacher-shortage.htm.

Hill, T. L. (2002). *No Child Left Behind policy brief: Teaching quality*. Denver: Education Commission of the States. www.ecs.org/clearinghouse/34/63/3463.pdf.

Hirsch, E. (2001, February). *Teacher recruitment: Staffing classrooms with quality teachers*. Denver: State Higher Education Executive Officers. www.sheeo.org/quality/mobility/recruitment.pdf.

Hoff, D. "New Orleans soliciting businesses for bonuses." *Education Week*, May 1, 2002. www.edweek.com/ew/newstory.cfm?slug=33recruit.h21.

Hoff, D. "Urban districts employing more aggressive hiring tactics." *Education Week*, October 3, 2001. www.edweek.com/ew/newstory.cfm?slug=05recruit.h21.

Holloway, L. "New York City campaigns to attract new teachers." *New York Times*, November 9, 1999.

H. R. 3889, *Teacher Tax Credit Act of 2002* (introduced in House). http://thomas.loc.gov/home/thomas.html.

H. R. 4599, *National Board-Certified Teachers in Low-Performing Schools Act of 2002* (introduced in House). http://thomas.loc.gov/home/thomas.html.

"Incentives and recruitment: Policy tables." In *Education Week*. (2000, January). "Quality Counts 2000: Who should teach?" www.edweek.com/sreports/qc00/tables/incentives-t1.htm.

Ingersoll, R. (2001, January). *Teacher turnover, teacher shortages, and the organization of schools*. Seattle: University of Washington, Center for the Study of Teaching and Policy. www.depts.washington.edu/ctpmail/PDFs/Turnover-Ing/-01-2001.pdf.

Johnston, R. "Chicago's efforts to recruit teachers pay off." *Education Week*, November 1, 2000. www.edweek.com/ew/ewstory.cfm?slug=09chicago.h20.

Johnston, R. "System thwarts teacher's bid to transfer to needy school." *Education Week*, July 11, 2001. www.edweek.com/ew/ewstory.cfm?slug=42teacher.h20.

Kirby, S. N., S. Naftel, and M. Berends. (1999). *Staffing at-risk school districts in Texas: Problems and prospects.* Santa Monica, CA: RAND. www.rand .org/publications/MR/MR1083/.

Kuriloff, A. "Proposal seeks relief for teachers: Many would be freed from income taxes." *The (New Orleans) Times-Picayune*, March 14, 2002. www.nola.com/education/t-p/index.ssf?/newsstory/r_johntax14.html.

Lankford, H., S. Loeb, and J. Wyckoff. (2002, Spring). Teacher sorting and the plight of urban schools: A descriptive analysis. *Educational Evaluation and Policy Analysis*, 24(1), 37–62.

Lee, J. (1998). "Teacher staffing and distribution patterns for 1997 in four Maryland LEAs." Paper presented at the Harvard Conference on Civil Rights and High Stakes K–12 Testing, December 4, 1998, New York. *In* Dezmon, B. (Ed.). (2001, January). *Minority achievement in Maryland at the millennium.* Report prepared by the Achievement Initiative for Maryland's Minority Students (AIMMS) Steering Committee. Baltimore: Maryland State Department of Education. www.msde.state.md.us/minority/pdf_files/2002/min.pdf.

Lippman, L., S. Burns, and E. McArthur. (1996, June). *Urban schools: The challenge of location and poverty.* NCES 96–184. Washington, D.C.: U.S. Department of Education, National Center for Education Statistics. www .nces.ed.gov/pubs/96184all.pdf.

Live Baltimore Marketing Center. "Baltimore City Employee Homeownership Program (BCEHP)." www.encorebaltimore.org/homebuy/bcehp.html.

Los Angeles Unified School District. "Los Angeles Teachers Mortgage Assistance Program." www.lausd.k12.ca.us/orgs/latmap/.

Markley, M. "Districts taking new steps to stem teacher turnover." *Houston Chronicle*, August 15, 2001.

Maryland State Department of Education. "Fact sheet 48: Quality Teacher Incentive Act." www.msde.state.md.us/fact%20sheets/fact48.html.

Maryland State Department of Education. "New incentives announced to attract and retain quality teachers." Press release, October 27, 1998. www.msde.state.md.us/pressreleases/1998/october/1998–1027b.html.

Maryland State Department of Education. "Teacher incentives update." www.msde.state.md.us/factsndata/IncentivesUpdateWeb.htm.

Maryland State Department of Education. "Teacher incentives update: Homeownership opportunities for teachers." www.msde.state.md.us/factsndata/ IncentivesUpdateWeb.htm.

Maryland State Education That Is Multicultural Advisory Council. (1998, September). *Minority achievement in Maryland: The state of the state.*

Baltimore: Maryland State Department of Education. www.msde.state. md.us/minority/pdf_files/minority.pdf.

Massachusetts Department of Education. "Deadline approaching for new teacher signing bonus program." Press release, January 23, 2002. www .doe.mass.edu/news/news.asp?id=487.

Massachusetts Department of Education. "Immediate changes to National Board program and Master Teacher program." Memorandum from David P. Driscoll, Commissioner of Education, to National Board certified teachers and candidates, June 12, 2002. www.doe.mass.edu/news/news.asp?id=772.

Massachusetts Department of Education. "The Massachusetts Institute for New Teachers (MINT): Overview." www.doe.mass.edu/mint/overview.html.

Massachusetts Department of Education. "Poor economy forces suspension of Master Teacher bonus program." Press release, June 13, 2002. www.doe .mass.edu/news/news.asp?id=771.

Mathews, J. "The smart money: In an effort to improve struggling schools offi- cials increasingly use financial bonuses to lure good teachers." *Washington Post*, April 10, 2001.

Mathews, J. "Virginia to trim teacher bonuses." *Washington Post*, November 20, 2001, p. B07.

McDermott, K. "House passes bill to give future teachers free tuition." *St. Louis Post-Dispatch*, April 2, 2002.

Miller, M. "A bold experiment to fix city schools." *The Atlantic*, July 1999. www.theatlantic.com/issues/99jul/9907vouchers.htm.

Nakamura, D., and C. A. Samuels. "In school, changes at the top: Area faces shortage of new principals." *Washington Post*, June 25, 2000, p. A01.

National Board for Professional Teaching Standards. "State and local action." www.nbpts.org.

National Center for Education Statistics. (1998). *The condition of education*. Washington, D.C.: U.S. Government Printing Office. Cited in Haycock, K. (2000, Spring). No more settling for less. *Thinking K–16, 4*(1), 3–12. Wash- ington, D.C.: The Education Trust.

National Commission on Teaching and America's Future. (2001, November/ December). "Doing it right: Anaheim City Schools have 100 percent fully certified teachers." *Focus on Teaching Quality, I*(4). www.nctaf.org/whatsnew/ FocusOnTeachingQuality_Dec2001.htm.

National Education Association. Internal memorandum, December 6, 2000.

National Education Association. *NEA 2000–2001 Resolutions: F/-9. Salaries and Other Compensation*. www.nea.org/resolutions/00/00f/-9.html.

National School Boards Association. "In Hartford, new teachers paid more than veterans." *School Board News*, July 17, 2001. www.nsba.org/sbn/01-jul/ 071701-2.htm.

National School Boards Association. "School districts cast global net to fill teacher positions." *School Board News*, January 11, 2000. www.nsba.org/sbn/00-jan/011100-3.htm.

NEA/NY (National Education Association, New York Affiliate). "NEA/NY applauds Senate plan to improve teacher quality." Press release, March 7, 2000. Statement by Gregory S. Nash, President, National Education Association of New York, NEA/NY. www.neany.org/pressrelease/030700.html.

New Visions for Public Schools. (1999, February). *Crisis in leadership: Finding and keeping educational leaders for New York City's public schools.* New York: Author. www.newvisions.org/resources/report4_1.shtml.

New York State Education Department. "Teachers of Tomorrow program information." www.highered.nysed.gov/kiap/TRDU/tot/totinfo.htm.

North Carolina Association of Educators. (2000, July). *Getting it right: Improving the ABC's of North Carolina.* ABC Survey Result Summary. www.ncae.org/news/abcsurvey/abcsurvey.shtml.

Odden, A., C. Kelley, H. Heneman, and A. Milanowski. (2001, November). "Enhancing teacher quality through knowledge- and skills-based pay." *CPRE Policy Briefs*, RB/-34. Philadelphia: University of Pennsylvania, Consortium for Policy Research in Education. www.cpre.org/Publications/rb34.pdf.

Office of the State Treasurer, California. "Extra Credit Teacher Home Purchase Program." www.treasurer.ca.gov/csfa/extracredit/details.htm.

Office of U.S. Representative Heather Wilson (R-NM). "Wilson aims to give teachers credit." Press release, March 8, 2002. http://wilson.house.gov/NewsCenter.asp.

Office of U.S. Representative Susan Davis (D-CA). "Susan Davis introduces bill on teacher quality." Press release, April 26, 2002. www.house.gov/susandavis/press/pr042602teacherquality.htm.

Office of U.S. Senator Jay Rockefeller (D-WV). "Making teachers a top priority, Rockefeller aims to support teacher certification and commitment to rural and low-income schools." Press release, August 1, 2002. http://rockefeller.senate.gov/2002/pr080102.html.

Olson, L. "Sweetening the pot." In *Education Week*. (2000, January). "Quality Counts 2000: Who should teach?" www.edweek.com/sreports/qc00/templates/article.cfm?slug=recruit.htm.

Pardington, S. "State denies a teaching crisis, except in poor school districts." *Contra Costa Times*, November 5, 2001.

Pardington, S. "State education study irks unions." *Contra Costa Times*, October 23, 2001.

Podgursky, M. (2001). "Regulation versus markets: The case for greater flexibility in the market for public school teachers." *In* Wang, M. C., and H. J.

Walberg. (Eds.). *Tomorrow's Teachers*, pp. 117–48. Richmond, CA: McCutchan Publishing Corporation.

Prince, C. (2002, January). *The challenge of attracting good teachers and principals to struggling schools*. Arlington, VA: American Association of School Administrators. www.aasa.org/issues_and_insights/issues_dept/challenges.htm.

Professional Development Task Force. (2001). *Learning . . . Teaching . . . Leading . . .: The Report of the Professional Development Task Force*. Sacramento: California Department of Education. http://goldmine.cde.ca.gov/cdepress/learnteachlead.pdf.

Public Law 107/-110, the *No Child Left Behind Act of 2001* [H. R. 1], Title II, Part A, Subpart 1, Section 2113(c)(12). www.ed.gov/legislation/ESEA02/pg21.html.

Public Law 107/-110, the *No Child Left Behind Act of 2001* [H. R. 1], Title II, Part A, Subpart 2, Sections 2123 (a)(2)(A); 2123 (a)(4)(C); and 2123 (a)(4)(D). www.ed.gov/legislation/ESEA02/pg22.html#sec2123.

Reid, K. S. "News in brief: A state capitals roundup. Hiring bonuses shot down in Neb." *Education Week*, June 6, 2001. www.edweek.com/ew/ewstory.cfm?slug=39caps.h20.

Robelen, E. W., and M. Walsh. "Bush proposal: Give tax credit for K–12 tuition." *Education Week*, February 13, 2002. www.edweek.com/ew/newstory.cfm?slug=22choice.h21.

Rossi, R. "Teacher woes worst in poor schools." *Chicago Sun-Times*, October 10, 2001. www.suntimes.com/output/news/cst-nws-teach10.html.

Rossi, R., B. Beaupre, and K. Grossman. "5,243 Illinois teachers failed key exams." *Chicago Sun-Times*, September 6, 2001. www.suntimes.com/output/news/cst-nws-main06.html.

Rossi, R., B. Beaupre, and K. Grossman. "Other states do it better." *Chicago Sun-Times*, September 9, 2001. www.suntimes.com/output/news/cst-nws-2main09.html.

Rossi, R., and D. McKinney. "Why are teacher tests secret? politicians ask." *Chicago Sun-Times*, September 7, 2001. www.suntimes.com/output/news/cst-nws-main07x.html.

S. 2844, *Incentives to Educate American Children (I Teach) Act of 2002* (introduced in Senate). http://thomas.loc.gov/home/thomas.html.

Sack, J. L. "Revenue shortfall prompts big school cuts in California." *Education Week*, February 6, 2002. www.edweek.com/ew/newstory.cfm?slug=21calif.h21.

"Scandalous education inequity." *The (San Jose) Mercury News*, editorial, August 8, 2002. www.bayarea.com/mld/mercurynews/news/opinion/3822673.htm.

"School employees get help with home buying." *Seattle Times*, March 27, 2002. http://seattletimes.nwsource.com/text/134426729_northshore27e.html.

Seymour, L. "SOL tests create new dropouts: Frustrated Virginia teachers switching courses, leaving public school." *Washington Post*, July 17, 2001, p. A01.

Shields, P. M., et al. (1999). *The status of the teaching profession: Research findings and policy recommendations. A report to the Teaching and California's Future Task Force*. Santa Cruz, CA: The Center for the Future of Teaching and Learning. www.cftl.org/publications.html.

Shields, P. M., et al. (2001). *The status of the teaching profession 2001*. Santa Cruz, CA: The Center for the Future of Teaching and Learning. www.cftl.org/documents/2001report/completereport.pdf.

South Carolina State Department of Education. "Teacher Specialist program." www.myscschools.com/offices/sq/tsos/.

Southeast Center for Teaching Quality. (2002, January). *Recruiting teachers for hard-to-staff schools: Solutions for the Southeast and the nation*. Chapel Hill, NC: Author. www.teachingquality.org/resources/pdfs/hard_to_staff_schools_regional_brief.pdf.

Spiri, M. H. (2001, May). *School leadership and reform: Case studies of Philadelphia principals*. Occasional papers. Philadelphia: University of Pennsylvania, Consortium for Policy Research in Education. www.cpre.org/Publications/children02.pdf.

State of Illinois, 92nd General Assembly Legislation, House Bill 0582. www.legis.state.il.us/legislnet/legisnet92/hbgroups/hb/920HB0582LV.html.

Strauss, R. (1998). *Teacher preparation and selection in Pennsylvania: Ensuring high performance classroom teachers for the 21st century*. (mimeo) Pittsburgh: Heinz School of Public Policy and Management, Carnegie-Mellon University.

Tapia, S. T. "Perks lure teachers with full credentials: Anaheim City offers extras, such as help with moving costs and student loans, to beef up its staff." *Orange County Register*, July 5, 2001.

Tennessee Advisory Commission on Intergovernmental Relations. (2000, February). "Teacher mobility among Tennessee school districts: A survey of causes." *TACIR Staff Research Briefs*, 6. www.state.tn.us/tacir/PDF_FILES/Education/Migration.pdf.

Urban Teacher Collaborative. (2000). *The urban teacher challenge: Teacher demand and supply in the Great City Schools*. Belmont, MA: Author. www.rnt.org/quick/utc.pdf.

U.S. Department of Education. "Cancellation/deferment options for teachers." www.ed.gov/offices/OSFAP/Students/repayment/teachers/index.html.

U.S. Department of Education. "Deferments for FFEL and Direct Loans." www.ed.gov/offices/OSFAP/Students/repayment/teachers/dlffel.html.

U.S. Department of Education. (2002, June 6). *Improving Teacher Quality state grants: Title II, Part A, non-regulatory draft guidance*. www.ed.gov/offices/OESE/SIP/TitleIIguidance2002.doc.

U.S. Department of Education. "Perkins Loan cancellation." www.ed.gov/offices/OSFAP/Students/repayment/teachers/perkins.html.

U.S. Department of Education. "Stafford Loan cancellation for teachers." www.ed.gov/offices/OSFAP/Students/repayment/teachers/stafford.html.

U.S. Department of Education. "Teaching reduced service requirement for Douglas Scholars." www.ed.gov/offices/OSFAP/Students/repayment/teachers/douglas.htm.

Useem, B. *In middle schools, teacher shortage reaches crisis levels*. www.philaedfund.org/notebook/Teacher%20Shortage.htm.

Viadero, D. "Philadelphia study: Teacher transfers add to educational inequities." *Education Week*, April 18, 2001. www.edweek.com/ew/ewstory.cfm?slug=31mobility.h20.

Viadero, D. "Researcher: Teacher signing bonuses miss mark in Mass." *Education Week*, February 21, 2001. www.edweek.com/ew/ewstory.cfm?slug=23bonus.h20.

Viadero, D. "Study: Teachers seek better working conditions." *Education Week*, January 9, 2002. www.edweek.com/ew/newstory.cfm?slug=16pay.h21.

"A visionary school plan in Maryland." *New York Times* editorial, April 30, 2002. www.nytimes.com/2002/04/30/opinion/_30TUE3.html?ex=1021187043&ei=1&en=f5ee07341313321c.

Watson, S. (2001, May). *Recruiting and retaining teachers: Keys to improving the Philadelphia Public Schools*. Philadelphia: University of Pennsylvania, Consortium for Policy Research in Education. www.cpre.org/Publications/children01.pdf.

Wells Fargo. "Wells Fargo Home Mortgage, CaHLIF and Freddie Mac address lack of affordable housing for California's teachers; announce new loan program." Press release, August 14, 2000. www.wellsfargo.com.

ABOUT THE AUTHOR

Cynthia Prince is an issues analysis director for the American Association of School Administrators. She is responsible for identifying and analyzing educational leadership issues to advance and support effective policies and practices in school systems nationwide. She has nearly 20 years of experience in education and language policy at the federal, state, and local levels. Previous positions held include coordinator of program evaluation for the Connecticut State Department of Education; chief of research, evaluation, and statistical services for the Maryland State Department of Education; and associate director for analysis and reporting for the National Education Goals Panel in Washington, D.C. She has authored numerous articles and research reports on teacher and principal quality, bilingual education, language policy, and education reform. She completed her undergraduate degree at Northwestern University and earned two master's degrees in education and in linguistics and a Ph.D. in education from Stanford University.